10/79

THE PET HOUSE BOOK

*Illustrations and diagrams by
Lura LaBarge
Projects built by George W. Beierle*

THE PET HOUSE BOOK

How To Build Housing, Accessories, and Playthings for Your Dogs, Cats, Birds, Lizards, Hamsters, and Other Pets

BY LURA LABARGE

Butterick Publishing

Because success and safety in working with materials and tools depend to a great extent on individual accuracy, skill, and caution, responsibility for any damage to property or injury to persons or animals related to the construction or use of the following projects must be assumed by the person building and using them.

Photographs by Robert Meyerriecks
Book design by Bobye G. List
Cover design by Winifred Young

Library of Congress Catalog Card Number: 76-56597
International Standard Book Number: 0-88421-031-6

To Leo M. and Leo R.

ACKNOWLEDGEMENTS

For their help in providing information and/or materials used in building the pieces shown on these pages, I want to thank Mr. Norman Pietros of the Homasote Company (Homasote®); Mr. P. C. Babb of Reynolds Metals (Reynolds Do-It-Yourself® Aluminum); and Mr. Harold Tamplin of Wellington Puritan Mills (cord for the cattrees). Mr. John R. Gill of Rohm and Haas (Plexiglas®), Mr. Charles Roth of Mail Order Plastics, and Mr. Karl Camp of AIN Plastics all offered helpful information on fabricating with acrylic sheet. Mr. Douglas J. Bennet of The Brewster Corporation was most encouraging about my use of their Timber-Topper® products.

I owe many thanks for all sorts of assistance and advice to Ms. Susan McDonough and her golden retriever Leo; to Ms. Lori and Ms. Tricia Price and their bassett hound Bertha; to Ms. Elizabeth Ruh and P. W. and the four gray kittens; to Ms. Fran Roberts, cats Beeb and Tassel, and K. C., the Wonder Dog; to Mr. Mike Romyns and Guinevere the gerbil; and to my son, Mr. Leo R. LaBarge, for securing the cooperation of his dog Pete.

I am indebted to Mrs. Ann Zummo of Sussex Aquarium and Pets for advice on building for all three rodent types; to Mr. Joseph Kemmerer of Little Pet for suggestions on behalf of the birds; and to Vern and Susan French of Small Worlds-Vivariums on the needs of amphibians and reptiles. Mr. and Mrs. French were most encouraging and informative in their comments about providing a healthy environment for Gerd and Ferd, the anoles; I am particularly thankful to Mr. Ralph deVries for planting the vivarium. Special thanks are also due Dr. William C. Gray, D.V.M., for the helpful suggestions he made regarding the care, safety, and health factors involved in designing for all the pets and for the time he spent reading the manuscript.

Again I want to thank Mr. George W. Beierle for his pleasant cooperation and good sense in translating my preliminary drawings into functioning finished projects. His comments often led to further simplification of construction details. Thanks are also due his daughter, Ms. Debbie Beierle, for her help in assembling many of the plastic projects; to our photographer, Mr. Robert Meyerriecks, for knowing how to get the best from our animal models; and to my editor, Ms. Willa Rosenblatt Speiser, for her patient prodding as well as her very competent editorial work.

CONTENTS

Introduction

LIKE HOUSE PLANS AND PROJECT BOOKS FOR humans, this is a book of do-it-yourself ideas for your pets. Not for them to do but for you to do for them.

We are concerned here with the family pet who is kept within your home or immediately outside it. Building for your friendly dog or cat is a little like fixing up a place for a visiting niece or nephew to stay. You may cater to a whim or two, but you make the rules; they share your world.

The family pet at the other extreme is the unpettable one to whom your world is inhospitable, if not downright hostile. Besides both salt- and fresh-water aquarium-dwellers, these include turtles, lizards, frogs, toads, and snakes. Furniture for the sit-and-look-at pet has to accommodate his tank or the case that contains a slice of his own environment—plus the accessory items necessary for maintaining it. This is the responsibility you assumed when you permitted him inside your home.

Between these two extremes are the cage birds and the rodents, whose popularity as pets has grown so rapidly in the past few years. Your environment can be made suitable with little trouble, but guinea pigs, hamsters, and gerbils haven't learned all the rules for living in your world. They require confinement that works both ways—protecting your world from their depredatory inclinations and protecting them from you. They deserve the best you can provide to make their lives in captivity healthy and fun-filled.

You're a friend to your dog or cat, kindly keeper to your rodents, and Nature to your turtle. One way or another, it is up to you to provide the things your pets need.

Just as there are many reasons for building your own home, so are there reasons for building things for your pets from a book such as this one. First, you'll find unique designs. By expending your own energy and creative talents you will be able to give your pet something special you could not buy for him. You'll also find it easier to adjust the dimensions of something you are about to build than to change the size of a finished object you've purchased ready made. We help you reason through the dimensions so that you can build the project you select to fit your pet and your home.

If cost is a factor, there are places where different materials or methods can safely be substituted for those we have used. There are also opportunities to select materials and/or methods that may better utilize your special talents as the builder. There are even choices you may wish to make on purely esthetic grounds. We mention these possibilities as they occur in outlining each project.

Construction in this book is geared to the average home craftsperson who enjoys building things, though of course you could hire a carpenter to build them for you. (Permission to mass produce an item from any of these designs is not automatically granted—that's a legal question.) All the projects are designed to be built with common hand tools and the popular power tools; they assume a general working knowledge of how to use those tools. A table saw (bench or radial) plus a band saw is ideal. A portable circular saw and/or a saber saw will save you time and effort. We include alternate details where necessary in case you have only hand tools to work with.

Because acrylic sheet and Do-It-Yourself® Aluminum require techniques with which you may not be familiar, we have included a section containing the manufacturer's tips for working these two materials. If you're not set up for them, it may be well to note here that they are workable with normal home-workshop tools and require very little in the way of special tools or equipment—and those quite inexpensive.

Before you start work, think about your pet's needs. Pets were animals before they were pets, wild before they were domesticated. They made their own housing before you took them on. They captured or found their own food before you guaranteed to provide it. They enjoyed the hunt and kept in shape keeping alive before you domesticated them. They lived in the wild before you assumed the responsibility for them. Even prize dogs and pedigreed cats have wild ancestors. Now that your pets are yours to feed and care for, you want to make them as happy as possible and they in turn will reward you in their own way.

First you'll want to read and learn about the life and habits of your pet. There are a lot of animal books available, many of them very well written and illustrated, designed for younger readers. Many general books the average pet owner comes across do not give complete, specific how-to-build-it information about the housing and accessories they suggest. There are books containing specifications for building kennels and row after row of cage-type hutches if you are raising show dogs or breeding laboratory animals. Easily available 4-H and USDA publications offer adequate information on housing horses, cows, sheep, goats, barnyard fowl, and other farm-type animals, but these are not pets. Narratives about wanderers from the wild who lived for a time with humans may well do more harm than good, though they are often interesting reading. The bibliography at the end of this book lists some books we have found noteworthy.

New pet owners need a good care-and-feeding book for the animals they have or are about to acquire. The best of these will give a good idea of what the normal animal needs to eat and drink, what bedding is suitable, what hours the animal keeps, what special environmental requirements must be maintained, what diseases to watch out for, and what inoculations might be needed. It will tell you what breeding and territorial habits may have a bearing on your choice of pet and will usually describe what toys are most suitable for the creature's natural activities. You'll find your own common sense a big help, too.

The advice of our local veterinarian has been helpful in establishing some basic ground rules for designing projects for pets. Dr. William C. Gray, D.V.M., suggests favoring designs and materials that promote easy cleaning. He has a word of warning on the matter of finishes—always use baby-safe paints, especially where the gnawing rodents are concerned. Location of cages is important, and temperature and humidity also require consideration. We've included anti-draft devices as Dr. Gray suggests, too. Space is important to confined animals, and you must consider the enclosed space/price ratio carefully before deciding to build the smallest possible case or cage. Understanding your pet is the first step in providing for its needs intelligently. Your own local veterinarian can help you start off in the right direction.

Large animal-feed producers have developed balanced diets for most domesticated animals, but do read up on your potential pet's eating habits before you accept a snake only to learn he eats nothing but live mice. Most animals drink water, but some lizards don't know it is water if it just sits there in a dish. They want their water moving or misted on plants.

Torn or shredded newspaper is suitable bedding for some animals but others, who eat it, find the ink does not agree with them. Watching a nocturnal animal all day for some sign of action is disappointing. Even hamsters are apt to be more active in the evening. Damp quarters are hard on most animals, as are drafts. Birds are quite susceptible to ills caused by damp perches, drafty cages, and lack of shelter from the sun. Many vivarium dwellers are very sensitive to too much heat or cold, too little or too much humidity. Fish have their own set of requirements— fresh-water or salt-water, depending on which is their normal world. And they are extremely touchy about heat and light conditions, too. Housekeeping chores vary widely from one animal to the next. Some of them put it all in the same place and some scatter it anywhere. Some are fastidious in their eating habits, others will tip over a water dish in nothing flat. Know what you're getting into and start with a healthy animal from a reputable pet dealer and the blessings of your local veterinarian.

For the sake of convenience and brevity, we refer to all pets as "he" in this book. Obviously pets are not all of one gender, and the use of one term of reference is in no way intended to imply that it is a male pet's world.

ONE

Getting Started

For a home-workshop person considering a project, the first questions are apt to be, "What am I going to build it out of?" and "What am I going to build it with?"

The builder of these projects may be an accomplished cabinetmaker or he may be your child anxious to make something for a pet. Our information is addressed to the experienced home craftsperson as well as the novice, to the person whose basement workshop has the capacity for turning out professional-quality Chippendale pieces as well as the apartment dweller whose shop is his tool tote. Obviously such diverse talents do not need exactly the same instructions, nor do they have the same collection of tools on hand. We try to tread a middle path—enough information for the inexperienced, coupled with suggested options to challenge the perfectionist semi-pro. We do assume a knowledge of basic woodworking techniques.

MATERIALS

The materials shown in these projects are all workable with the hand and power tools found in the average home workshop. If you don't have any power tools, don't worry. All the projects *can* be built with hand tools alone. Most of the parts are wood, with hardboard where flat, thin pieces are called for and plywood where something a bit thicker is required. On one design, Homasote® is shown, while many of the ideas are best worked out in acrylic sheet (Plexiglas®, Acrylite®, etc.), others in Do-It-Yourself® Aluminum.

Some materials are obvious choices: where a frame of sorts is to be constructed, it is more logical to choose four long, skinny pieces of solid wood than to cut up a sheet of plywood. Throwing away the center to use the frame that is left is wasteful. Plywood is the answer of first choice where a solid panel of reasonable strength is what you want, though you can build up a solid panel by using parallel boards with cleats across to hold them together. Selecting the panel-shaped material obviously entails less work. Hardboard and acrylic sheet have the "panel"

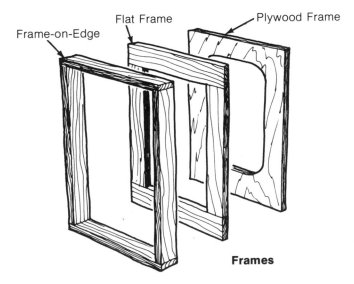

Frame-on-Edge   Flat Frame   Plywood Frame

Frames

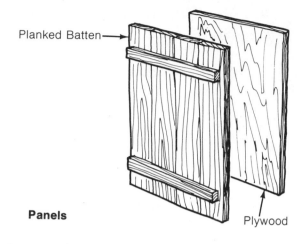

Planked Batten

Plywood

Panels

quality plus other features that, for some jobs, make them first choice.

Not quite so obvious, but easily understood is the idea of making a panel by "filling in" a frame—with perforated or expanded aluminum, or hardware cloth (woven galvanized wire), or even plastic film too thin to be a "panel" by itself. We've made some of these decisions for you in the projects shown. You could make a vivarium case by building a box frame and inserting glass or thin plastic sides. We made ours by selecting a transparent panel material ($\frac{1}{4}$"-thick acrylic sheet) strong

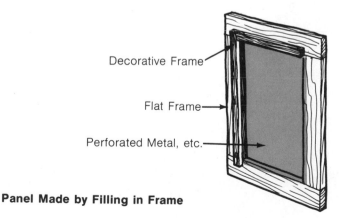

Decorative Frame

Flat Frame

Perforated Metal, etc.

Panel Made by Filling in Frame

enough to be self-supporting. You could make the cat carrier by using a panel material like hardboard or plywood and drilling holes through it to provide the air circulation necessary. We chose to insert perforated Do-It-Yourself Aluminum® in front and end frames.

There are several questions to ask yourself when choosing the material you want to use. Will it work? Can you afford it? Can you get it? Is it available in an economical size? Can you make it do what you want it to? Is it durable in the use you plan? How easy is it to clean? And most important, how is it affected by the animal concerned and how will the material affect the animal?

Sometimes a special quality is what you seek. Will this size mesh restrain that size animal? Will the perforations in this pattern provide enough air movement? Will this transparent material provide visibility good enough to observe the life that goes on behind it? If insulation is important, as it is in a dog-house, that may be the basis for choice. Which material provides the best insulation value for the least amount of money? Or your choice may hinge on a whim—do you like the texture of painted Homasote® better than that of inexpensive stained plywood?

In almost any project you build in a home shop, the question of cost enters. There are often alternative materials that can be used, sometimes by simple substitution of one material for another or by simple alterations in detail. At other times, it may take an alternative solution to the original problem. In some applications, salvage materials can be used, but you must be wary. Crate lumber is apt to be splintery and perhaps full of knot holes. These flaws are usually acceptable where they do not materially reduce the strength of a piece of wood beyond usable qualifications, but a board with a knothole in it is not a reasonable choice to enclose a gerbil, who can easily crawl through the hole.

Durability is another factor to consider. We used $\frac{1}{8}$"-thick colored acrylic sheet in our rodent projects. The rodents will eat it eventually, as they would eat ⅛"-thick painted hardboard. Acrylic sheet won't kill them and it looks better during destruction than fuzzy, scratched, and paint-chipped hardboard. You could build their toys of corrugated cardboard, for nothing, and make new ones every week if cost is really your deciding factor. Another choice went the other way. Expanded aluminum makes very attractive cages, but rodents can gnaw their way out. We opted here for the less attractive but also less destructible hardware cloth, which is also less expensive. Common sense will help you select materials, sometimes from pieces you have on hand; or you can follow our suggestions and use the materials we show.

TOOLS

Throughout this book, we describe how these projects were built. Most home craftspersons know pretty well what jobs the tools they have will do. They understand what is necessary and prudent to gain any specific result. In many how-to books, there are lists of tools required to build each project. Our feeling is that, while certain tools will make some particular jobs easier, listing them as "necessary" is a bit strong. Where there is a preferred or recommended tool or method, we will suggest it, but for the most part, use your head and the tools you have. A vise is nice but C-clamps will hold bar stock while you cut it, too.

Assuming a middle range in the way of tools, you'll have a square and something to measure and mark with. Hand or power, you have sawing capabilities for both straight cuts and curved ones. There are a few holes to drill, some edges to smooth, joints in wood to glue and nail, but very few screws to drive. For acrylic pieces, you may need to secure a dispenser for the solvent adhesive and to lay in a supply of masking tape. There's a special hand tool for scribe-and-break straight cuts in acrylic if you don't have the proper power saw blade. For the aluminum, heavy duty shears will cut the perforated or expanded pieces. You can use a utility knife and a metal straight edge for straight cuts on plain aluminum sheet. We assume you know how to hit a nail, hold a saw, use a drill, and drive a screw. We have to assume that if you have the tool, you know how to operate it. If it is so new that you don't know, you will still have the operator's manual that came with it. Think through each project you want to make, in the light of the materials shown and the tools you have.

There is one place where the lack of a bench saw or radial power saw may throw you. Since the rabbeting operation is beyond the capacity of many saws, alternate details are provided.

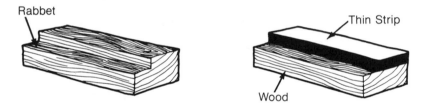

Rabbet

In theory, it is a simple exchange; merely replace the rabbeted piece with two pieces. A colonial craftsperson might have used chisels or a molding plane to handcut the groove, but today, if we cannot do a particular job easily and quickly, we redesign the job.

You'll undoubtedly find other such places where your own ingenuity can overcome any lack of fancy tools. For example, without a miter box, it's hard to make mitered joints by hand, but butt-jointed frames hold screening material in place, too. You'll need scratch paper and good sharp pencils with erasers for the calculations necessary to make any given project fit your tools, your materials, and your pet.

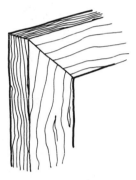

Miter Joint

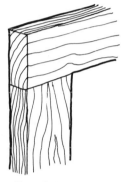

Butt Joint

ACRYLIC

First, to set the record straight, Plexiglas® is the registered trade name of the Rohm and Haas Company; Acrylite® is the registered trade name of the American Cyanamid Company. The generic term for this thermoplastic is "acrylic sheet."

Acrylic sheet is a self-supporting panel material and, in many ways, simpler to build with in the home shop than glass is. We have used clear or colorless transparent acrylic sheet $\frac{1}{4}$" thick where we want visibility along with confinement. The appeal of bright color that goes all the way through the material makes the $\frac{1}{8}$"-thick color sheet our choice for toys and accessories. Many glaziers carry the transparent sheet for safety glazing, and it is all available by mail order. (See the suppliers list at the end of this book.)

Acrylic sheet can be worked with normal hand and power tools. As a general rule, leave the protective paper or film on as long as possible, because acrylic sheet gets scratched easily.

To make straight cuts by hand, use a Plastic Plus™ or a Red Devil® Cutting Tool for Plexiglas. Scribe the line along a straight edge. Run the tool five or six times over the line on the $\frac{1}{8}$"-thick material, eight or ten times on the thicker stuff. Break along the scored line, holding the material over a $\frac{3}{4}$" dowel, in pretty much the same way as you score and break glass.

To cut acrylic sheet with power saws, use a blade with at least fourteen teeth per inch in a saber saw, at least ten per inch in a band saw. In a circular saw, a blade recommended for finish cuts in plywood and laminated plastics is fine. Don't force the feed.

A hand drill fitted with a regular bit meant for metal works well if you go slow and back up your work firmly. Use a special-purpose high-speed twist drill recommended for drilling acrylic sheet if you drill with power. It's best to avoid screw fastenings as much as possible, because acrylic expands and contracts with temperature changes.

Edges that will be seen need to be finished neatly. File with a fine-toothed metal file, then sand. On the transparent acrylic, finally use a "wet or dry" 150–220 grit sandpaper, then buff with a cloth wheel and buffing compound. Finish up with more buffing, using a clean cloth wheel for a sparkling clear edge.

The big difference between putting together pieces of acrylic sheet and putting together pieces of anything else is in using the solvent adhesive. Beware—the solvent is flammable, and toxic if inhaled or swallowed. Reasonable care in its use is prudent and a well-ventilated area a necessity.

The adhesive has a long chemical name, but if you ask for "solvent adhesive for acrylic sheet," you'll get what you want. It dissolves the plastic on contact, traveling along the joint by capillary action. A little practice will give you confidence. Using the applicator sold by distributors of the product is the easiest way to get it where you want it, though a syringe or an oil can with a fine spout will also work. Don't polish the surfaces to be joined, just make sure they are clean. Take off the protective paper or film and hold the pieces in position with masking tape preparatory to running the adhesive in. Think first and you'll do neat work. Remember, gravity is on your side. There are projects where a wood block can be used to advantage to space two pieces to be joined to a third piece or to give you a square corner to tape two pieces to. You need to tape the pieces so the surfaces to be joined stay put as the solvent works and the joint dries completely.

On bending acrylic sheet—we originally designed some of these projects for a formed corner, that is, one requiring a right-angle bend. However, this takes a strip heater which, though it is simple enough (the electrical parts come as a package, you build a supporting frame), is quite a bit to construct just to get more easily cleaned corners in your rodent cage. If you already work with plastics, you will know that right-angle joints shown as glued joints might, alternatively, be formed. In our opinion, it is simply not worth the trouble or expense to make a strip heater for two bends.

ALUMINUM

One of the materials used in some of these projects is Reynolds Do-It-Yourself® Aluminum. You'll find sheets of this material at larger hardware and building-materials suppliers, especially those catering to a do-it-yourself trade. Plain or textured sheet is available in natural aluminum, while perforated sheet (in three patterns) also comes gold anodized. Expanded aluminum ("Decorative Panels") in three other patterns is available in three finishes—natural, gold, and black.

Use a scriber for marking accurately, a fine-line felt-tipped pen if you want to see the marks. Long, straight cuts on plain sheet are easily made with a utility knife guided along a straightedge, clamped in place. Score and then break the sheet. Heavy duty kitchen shears or tin snips can also be used. On all cuts you will want to use a knife or a file to take the sharp edges off. Do this as soon as the cuts are made and you'll save yourself getting scratched or cut.

To bend flat sheet, you will need a pair of straight boards. Clamp the sheet between them, at the line where you want the bend to be. Using the boards and keeping the rest of the sheet flat on the workbench, make the bend. If you want a sharp corner, fasten the wood strip sandwich to your bench with C clamps and, using another wood block, hammer on it along the folded corner. You will be able to make a quite sharp bend this way.

In working with the perforated and expanded patterns, scissors, shears, or tin snips work better than the utility knife for cutting to size. In our designs the raw edges are always covered with a wood strip.

To paint plain aluminum, prepare the surface by sanding very lightly with a fine grit paper or by etching clean with an appropriate metal-cleaning jelly. Then wash with detergent, rinse, and wipe down with lacquer thinner. Use a primer and a finish paint meant for aluminum.

In cutting bar stock, use a hacksaw or a crosscut saw with at least eleven teeth to the inch. If you have a power saw, it will take a fine-toothed blade to do a good job. Always protect the surface of the stock by using a pad of scrap wood. To bend bar stock, as for the dog shelf, you will need a jig. Form each bend by hand, using the jig, then hammer with a wooden or rubber mallet or with your claw hammer and a block of wood. For the holes, make a tiny indentation at the center of where you want a hole drilled, so the drill gets started at that point. You'll find that the Do-It-Yourself® Aluminum is soft enough that you can easily put a rounded corner on where it makes sense. Always knock off sharp burrs with a rasp or a file as you work.

BUILD TO FIT AND FIT TO BUILD

Building for pets is actually no different from building for human animals. The project you build should fit its occupant or user and make the best use of the materials in the sizes available to you.

In each project we give you some suggested dimensions and show you where you can deviate from these few "musts" easily. Places where size matters most are where the animal and the project make close contact. Places like doorways are typical examples of this. Although most types of pet come in a more or less standard size, some kinds run a wider range. Your gerbil is apt to be pretty much the same size as the one next door, but you'll want to measure your dog for any project you build for him to use. All dogs are far from being the same size. He won't mind dropping his head a bit, but crouching on all fours to enter his own dog house is a bit much.

For most caged pets, making something an inch or two bigger or smaller won't matter. But given a choice, make the bigger. The bird flight cage we made to take advantage of stock-size expanded aluminum. Sheets are 24″ x 48″. If you don't want to use aluminum sheets and can only get 28″-wide woven wire, the birds will be happy with the wider cage, though it won't be nearly as attractive.

The manner in which we dimension the drawings to come allows for a greater flexibility in the cross-sectional size of the wood strips required. Whatever size screen mold you have on hand will work. If you rip 1 x 3's in half instead of buying two 1 x 2's, things will work out just as well. Again, where size is important is where the animal is in close contact.

You need to know your pet to see which dimensions make the difference. Birds are touchy about their feet. The diameter of wood perches makes a difference. Birds' feet grasp $\frac{3}{8}$″ to $\frac{5}{8}$″ diameter wood dowels best. $\frac{1}{4}$″ and $\frac{3}{4}$″ diameter will work, but a piece of closet poling $1\frac{3}{8}''$ in diameter just won't do, and an $\frac{1}{8}''$ dowel that is over $2''$ long will bend under the weight of only one parakeet. Naturally, if you're housing a parrot or a macaw, who has bigger feet, you will consider his claw size in your design.

You need to think, too, in choosing the projects to build, whether or not they suit your pet psychologically. A cat who's scared of heights is not going to climb a cattree. You need to know not only how big your pet is and how big he is likely to become, but what sort of things he does or would do if you provided the equipment. Obviously, no project should be constructed in such a way that it could harm your pet. Anything you build should be comfortable, suitable, workable, cleanable—and fun for you and your pet. Working it out may mean more arithmetic for you, but it means a custom-made project for your pet, as unique as your pet is.

TWO

Projects

DOGS

Keeping a dog is a lot easier if you have a place for everything, including the dog. The projects in this section will help. To give you a good start, we've begun with the simpler projects.

If it's a new puppy you want to build something for, the dog shelf, fully equipped with a leash, harness or collar, shampoo, and brush or comb, makes a nice gift for the new owner. Throw in a good care-and-feeding book and you give the new puppy and owner both a good start.

Any dog outdoors for more than a leashed walk needs a water dish handy. If your dog is like most, tipping the dish over is the most natural thing in the world. The one we show you how to make is simplicity itself. A simple dowel keeps it on the stake, easy to remove for daily cleaning. Occasionally you may find a dog who is confused and thinks he is a beaver, but mostly dogs do more damage to your things than to their own. To be on the safe side, don't paint the stake. The stake will be subjected to water and wear and tear and will look shoddy rather quickly if it is painted. (Any pet items you do paint should be done with non-toxic coatings, of course.)

Dogs do get to be part of the family, but they have to know

where they stand. If yours is an outdoor dog who needs a doghouse, don't confuse him by letting him sleep indoors some of the time. If yours is an indoor dog, he hardly needs a doghouse. If he's an indoor dog who goes outdoors for a few hours at a time, either tied or in a fenced yard, he needs patio-type accommodations. You know from observation that, given a choice, he will sleep in the sun on top of the picnic table on a fairly cold winter day if the wind isn't too strong. So a wood deck with a windscreen is a logical sun spot for him. Spring and fall, he'll like the dry surface of the wood, perhaps without the windscreen. Summer, if the deck is in the shade, he may enjoy the cooling results of any breeze that gets beneath it—but don't be surprised if on really hot days he still prefers a freshly dug hole in the cooler earth. You would too. Go feel how hot wood gets in 95° sun.

If you want to build a doghouse, remember that animals in the wild move around and choose their own bedrooms with light and air in mind. When you supply the house for your outdoor dog, you do the choosing. There is some controversy about the size of a doghouse in relation to the size of the dog. Should it be big enough to move around in or small enough to conserve body heat? In most climates, both are desirable—room to stretch out in summer and closer-fitting space in the winter. This suggests a removable draft partition or baffle.

There are some things to bear in mind about doghouses generally. Keep them up off the ground, both to lessen the chance of early wood rot and to provide a warmer floor in winter. It's a good idea to have some means of ventilating the sleeping quarters. A panel that can be removed when you are cleaning the interior is also advisable. Don't use metal or linoleum on the floor. It gets too cold, unless you are really scrupulous in furnishing sufficient litter material.

Whatever you build, do it with the dog in mind. What's easiest and most pleasant for him will pretty nearly always turn out to be easiest and most pleasant for you, too.

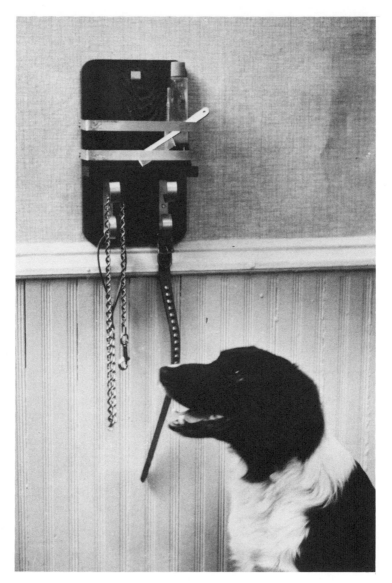

First, decide what you are going to keep on the shelf. Measure those things and see how big a shelf you need to make. The shelf shown here is sized to hold shampoo, flea powder, brush, and comb. Leash, collar, and an indoor-outdoor dog's towel hang on the hooks below. You may prefer to make a shelf for your pet's "reward" food and a special toy, with hooks below for harness, leash and coat. Our design shows aluminum bar stock. You may want a simpler, all-wood shelf with brass coat hooks below for leash and collar or harness. Once you understand the basic idea of making a shelf, styling details are a matter of choice.

To duplicate the shelf shown, you will need a 1 x 8, 14″ long, and a piece of 1 x 4 cut to the same length as the 1 x 8 is wide. Clear white pine would be nice, but you can use whatever you have long enough scraps of. You'll need one 6′ length of ⅛″ x ¾″ Do-It-Yourself® Aluminum bar stock and ten #3 wood screws, ⅝″ long (flat-headed look best but require countersinking the bar stock; round-headed screws are fine), and one screw long enough to mount the hanger hook to your wall. We used a wiped-on oil stain plus wax to finish the wood.

1-1 Make the Hanger Hook first. (See the section in chapter 1 on working with aluminum, if you've never used it before.) You will need to use a jig. A jig is simply something to bend stock around. Mark the Backboard for a rectangular hole to clear the front leg of the Hanger Hook you bend.

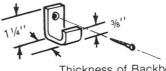

Thickness of Backboard Plus $\frac{1}{16}''$

1-1 Hanger Hook

1-1 Detail
Bracket Hooks

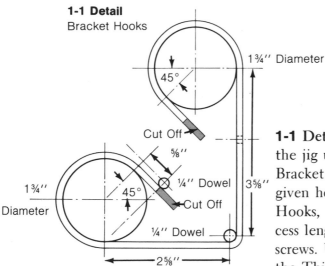

1-1 Detail Dimensions for the jig used to bend the Bracket Hooks shown are given here. Bend the Bracket Hooks, then cut off the excess length and drill for the screws. Use the Shelf plus the Thickness of the Backboard to lay out a jig for bending the two Keeper Straps. Drill the mounting holes.

1-2

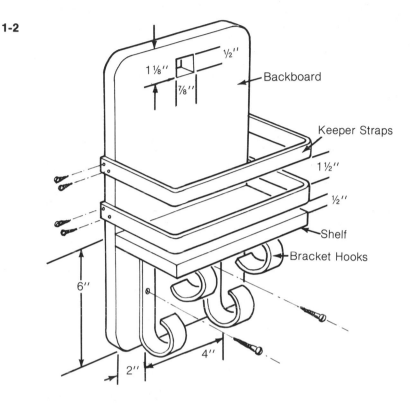

Backboard

1 1/8''

1/2''

7/8''

Keeper Straps

1 1/2''

1/2''

Shelf

Bracket Hooks

6''

2''

4''

1-2 To assemble the shelf, first complete the Backboard. Drill and shape the hole you marked for the Hanger Hook and round off the corners. Glue and nail through Backboard into Shelf. When glue has hardened, apply wood finish. Then, Keeper Straps in position, mark edges of Backboard for drilling pilot holes. Do the same for the Bracket Hook mounting holes. Attach Keeper Straps and Bracket Hooks. Install the Hanger Hook where you want the shelf to hang.

Hang up the shelf and fill it. Teach your dog to sit quietly under the shelf when you go there to get his leash to take him for a walk. He can learn to do that each time you say "Want to go for a walk?" if you say the same thing in the same way each time and let him know what you expect him to do. When he does it right, you take him out. Soon he may get the idea and go sit under the shelf to tell you he wants to go for a walk.

OUTDOOR WATER DISH   Project 2
(see also color plate 2)

The advantage of this project is that you can remove the dish for cleaning without uprooting the stake. Remember to clean it often. To make this project, you'll need a tube or bundt cake pan or a gelatine mold that can be set over a stake as shown. (The angel cake pans that come apart aren't too successful because they leak as soon as they get bent, so look for a one-piece model.) In addition you'll need a pole or broom handle that will go through the hole in the tube pan and can be sharpened to drive into the ground, and two short dowels small enough in diameter to go through the stake. If you have a wooden Bead that will fit the dowel, it makes a nice handle. You will also need two doughnut-shaped rings cut from scrap wood, plywood, or hardboard.

2-1 Secure the Pan first. This is a mark-as-you-go project and depends on how the pieces fit the Stake. The top or Keeper Ring should be pinned about 1″ down from the top of the Stake. The Bottom Ring will either fit up inside the tube, if you make it that small, or serve as a circular shelf on which to set the pan, if you make it larger. In either place, make its center hole a tight fit on the Stake. Figure out where to drill the hole for the Dowel Pin just below the Bottom Ring. Drill it and set the ring down in place. Put the Pan on. Put the Top Ring on (make the center hole in it a loose fit on the Stake.) Mark where to drill for the top Dowel Pin. Take the Pan and Top Ring off to get them out of your way and drill a hole 90° (a quarter of the way around the stake) from the first one. Using a block of wood to protect the top of the Stake, drive it into the ground

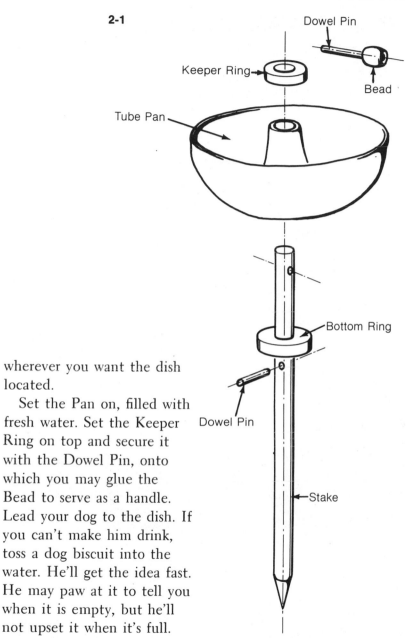

2-1

Dowel Pin

Keeper Ring

Bead

Tube Pan

Bottom Ring

Dowel Pin

Stake

wherever you want the dish located.

Set the Pan on, filled with fresh water. Set the Keeper Ring on top and secure it with the Dowel Pin, onto which you may glue the Bead to serve as a handle. Lead your dog to the dish. If you can't make him drink, toss a dog biscuit into the water. He'll get the idea fast. He may paw at it to tell you when it is empty, but he'll not upset it when it's full.

YEAR-ROUND DECK   Project 3

(see also color plate 2)

The deck we show is designed for a middle-sized dog. It has a detachable windscreen. A really big dog might prefer something a bit larger (add 6″ in width, another 12″ or 18″ in length for the easiest arithmetic.) A tiny dog—say a toy terrier—could do with a 12″ high windscreen and a half-size platform. If your dog will cooperate, have him lie, fully extended, on a piece of paper you've cut to 30″ x 36″ to get a good idea of how much room he'll have. Be generous about the deck size. Remember, you might want to sit on the deck beside your dog as you comb him out after his bath.

3-1 If the overall size of your Deck is to be 36″, cut the Decking (we used 1 x 4) to equal 36″ less twice the thickness of the material you'll use for the Edge Frame. Lay out the slats as you cut them on a level surface, spacing them with dimes or matchbook covers to make even spaces between them. When the total is about 27″ to 29″, you have cut enough. Measure it exactly and cut three Cleats to that length. Glue and nail the Decking to the three Cleats, making sure you have the Cleats parallel and the Decking on it squarely, spacing the Decking as you did before. Make sure the ends of the Decking and the surface of the end Cleats are all flush. Enclose the assembly in the Edge Frame, keeping this Frame-on-Edge flush with the tops of the Decking.

3-1

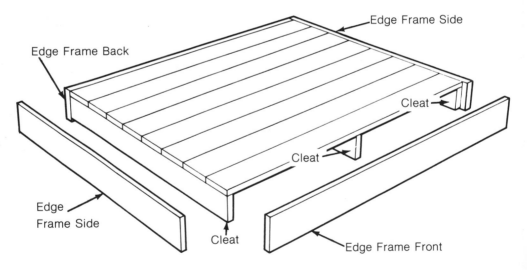

3-2 Turn the Deck assembly over and attach four Legs with glue and nails or screws. The length of the legs depends a bit on the size of the dog and what sort of ground you have. Try to get the bottom of the platform close enough to the ground so the dog can't easily get under it and far enough above the ground so the earth will dry out underneath. There's no law that says the four legs have to be equal lengths. If you're faced with sloping terrain, though, longer stakes, sharpened and set into the earth more permanently, might be a better solution.

3-2

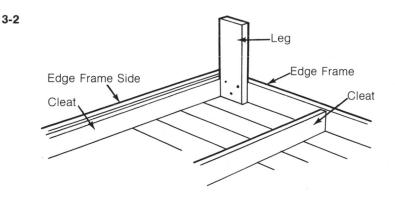

Leg

Edge Frame Side

Edge Frame

Cleat

Cleat

3-3 To make the Wind-screen, you will need to frame two pieces of acrylic sheet so they can be bolted to the platform. We did that by making a Flat Frame of 1 x 2's, rabbeting the Inner Frame to receive the acrylic.

Arithmetic: Length of Wind-screen Frame equals width of Platform.

Cut Outer Frame Top and Bottom to that length.

Cut Inner Frame Top and Bottom to that length less twice the width of the material used for Inner Frame Sides.

Acrylic Sheet $\frac{1}{4}''$ thick needs to be set so that it is held in a groove about $\frac{1}{2}''$ deep all around with clearance of $\frac{1}{8}''$ top and sides. Therefore rabbet Inner Frame members $\frac{1}{2}''$ x $\frac{1}{4}''$.*

Length of Acrylic Sheet will equal length of Inner Frame Top or Bottom plus $\frac{3}{4}''$. If width of Acrylic Sheet is 18'', length of Inner Frame Side will be 18'' minus $\frac{7}{8}''$, plus the width of the Top and Bottom members.

Assemble Inner Frame and double check size before cutting acrylic. Glue and clamp Frame and set in the acrylic sheet. Cut Outer Frame members so Top is equal to full length of Frame, and Outer Frame Sides will equal frame height less twice width of Outer Frame material. Glue and nail Outer Frame to Inner Frame, adding Bolting Skirt as shown.

If you did not use redwood, apply finish to all the wood parts *before* inserting the acrylic, as some finishes damage the plastic.

Alternate: If you don't have power tools, a $\frac{1}{4}''$ thick Hardboard strip can be used on each Inner Frame member to build up a cross section that will do the same thing the rabbeted strips do. Just size your strips so a setback $\frac{1}{2}''$ wide is left to retain the Acrylic Sheet and everything else is the same. Glue and nail the Hardboard Strips to the Frame members.

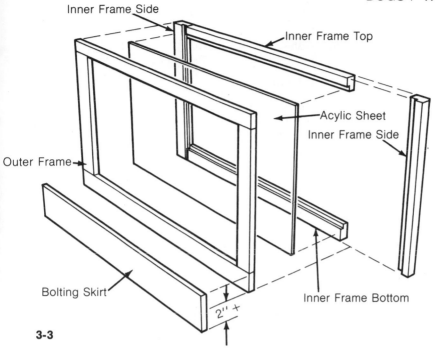

Inner Frame Side

Inner Frame Top

Acylic Sheet

Inner Frame Side

Outer Frame

Bolting Skirt

Inner Frame Bottom

2" +

3-3

3-3 Alternate

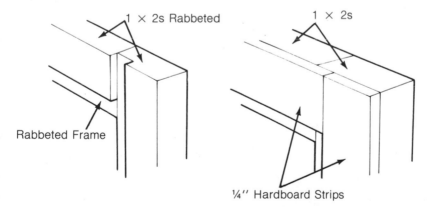

1 × 2s Rabbeted

1 × 2s

Rabbeted Frame

¼" Hardboard Strips

3-4 However you built the
End Windscreen Frame, the
Back Frame is done the
same way except the length
is equal to the length of the
platform minus the total
thickness of the End Frame.
Make the Back Skirt longer
than the Platform by the
thickness of the End Bolting
Skirt material, as indicated.

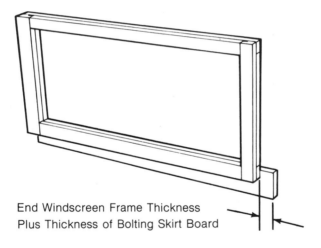

End Windscreen Frame Thickness
Plus Thickness of Bolting Skirt Board

3-4 Back Windscreen

3-5 To assemble the Windscreen, clamp the End and Back Frames on the platform and drill for $\frac{1}{4}''$-diameter Carriage Bolts or machine screws long enough to accommodate a Washer and Wing Nut. Connect the two Windscreen Frames at the top with a $2\frac{1}{2}''$ or $3''$ metal Corner Brace.

Set the deck where you want it, angling it so the Windscreen will take the prevailing winter winds. Make your dog understand that this is where he is to sun himself, not on the picnic table and not in the middle of the flower bed.

3-5

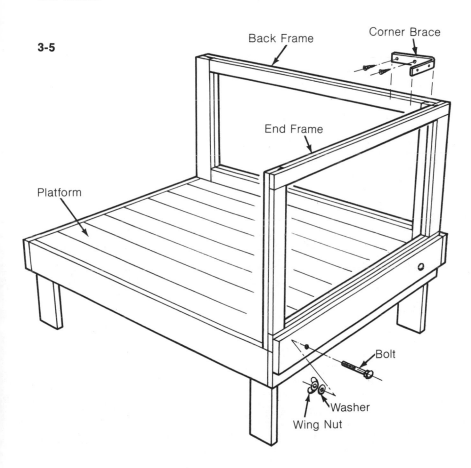

Back Frame

Corner Brace

End Frame

Platform

Bolt

Washer

Wing Nut

DOGHOUSE Project 4

(see also color plate 1)

This is a conventional frame doghouse with 2 x 4's for floor and roof framing, 2 x 3's for walls, and Homasote® for surfacing both interior and exterior. If you use hardboard or ¼″ plywood, you will probably want to add insulation within the walls and roof as well as under the floor. We have simply panelized the construction somewhat for easier handling in the home workshop. If you're an experienced carpenter, you won't need all the 1, 2, 3 instructions. If you're not all that experienced, you'll find the step-by-step information breaks it down into manageable units for you. Whatever your experience, read the whole project through first, with scratch paper and a measuring device of some sort handy.

To make a doghouse (or anything else) fit your dog, you first need to know how big your dog is. Make a note of his body Length, Height at shoulders, and broadest Width. As a quick double-check, catch him curled up asleep to determine a comfortable "average space required for sleeping." To determine a few key dimensions, follow through on this arithmetic:

The overall length of the doghouse is equal to the dog's Length plus one-third of his Length plus two times the total thickness of a wall. For the dog shown, that's 39″ plus 13″ plus 7¼″. That is 59¼″; rounded off to the nearest even inch it is 60″, or 5′. We figure a wall ½″ for interior Homasote®, 2⅝″ for the width of a 2 x 3, and ½″ for the Homasote® on the exterior.

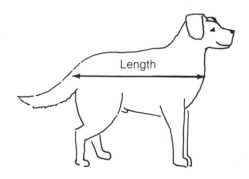

Length

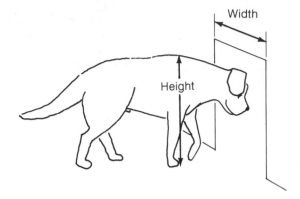

The overall width is equal to the dog's Height at the shoulder plus half that figure plus two walls. For this dog, that is 24″ plus 12″ plus 7¼″, or 43¼″, rounded off to 44″.

For the height of the Back Wall Panel, figure the dog's Height plus ⅓ that figure. For this dog, that is 24″ plus 8″, or 32″.

You'll want the shed-style Roof to slope at least 1″ in every 12″. (Stated properly, that's a roof pitch of one on twelve.) For you it means that if the overall width is 36″, the height of the Front Wall Panel should be 3″ more than that of the Back Wall Panel. For every 3″ more in front-to-back dimension add ¼″ more in height to the Front Wall Panel. We made the Front Wall Panel 3¾″ higher than the Back.

For the Doorway, add 2″ to your dog's Height and a total of 4″ to his Widest dimension for the finished opening size. We added 2″ to 24″ and 4″ to 13″ for an opening that, when it was finished, was 26″ high by 17″ wide.

To create a vestibule that will help shelter your dog in bad weather, build a Baffle Panel. The Baffle Panel needs to be mounted to a stud; this means the passage will be a bit wider than the doorway. The Baffle Panel should be at least half the width of the inside of the doghouse. Ours is 18″ wide and sets so the passage is about 22″ wide.

The space cut off by the Baffle should be comfortably larger than the "average sleeping space" occupied by your pet but not so much larger that he'll get cold.

We suggest you record your figures. The dog won't check up on your mathematics but you'll need the numbers, first to get your lumber list organized, then to cut parts to length. For instance, six sheets of Homasote® were enough to complete this size doghouse only by piecing the ceiling. Some of the trim is made of scraps of hardboard ¼″ thick left from another job. See what you have on hand that might be suitable in one place or another first. Study the whole project with this in mind before you order anything.

Longest Dimension Asleep

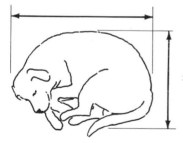

Shortest Dimension Asleep

4-1 Floor Frame Use 2 x 4's to make the Floor Frame. Cut the Rim Joists to equal the overall Length you figured minus two times the thickness of the exterior surfacing material you will use. Cut all other Joists to equal the outside Width minus the thickness of the two Rim Joists and two times the thickness of the exterior surfacing material. Space the Joists 16″ apart center to center, as far as possible, so you'll only have to adjust one piece of insulation. Both roll and batt forms of insulation come in standard widths suitable for this spacing. Glue and nail the Floor Frame as shown, making sure it is squared up and trued.

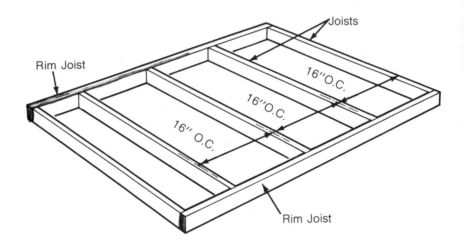

4-1

4-2 **Floor Platform**   Cut
Plywood Floor accurately to
fit the Floor Frame flush on
all four sides. Nail it in
place, spacing nails along all
the Joists evenly, 6″ to 8″
apart.

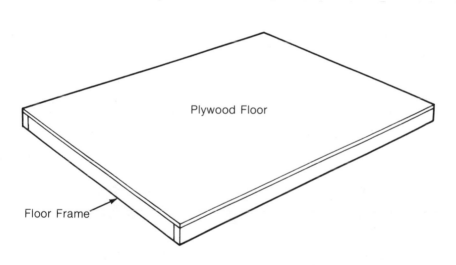

Plywood Floor

Floor Frame

4-2

4-3 Front Wall Frame Use
the Floor Platform just
formed as a work surface on
which to frame the walls.
Sills and Plates for the Front
and Back Walls are all the
same length as the Length of
the Floor Platform. The
length of the Studs for the
Front Wall equals the
Height of the Front Wall
Panel (which you just figured
out a few pages ago) minus
the thickness of Sill and
Plate. You will need to make
a rough opening for the
Doorway.

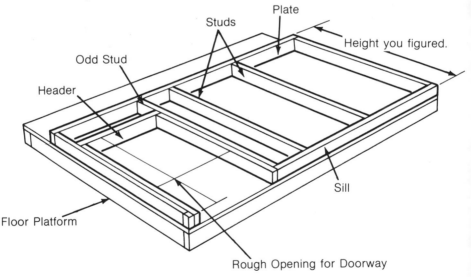

4-3

4-3 Detail   The easy way to do that is to run Plate and Sill the full Length of the Wall Frame. To locate the Odd Stud, add two times the thickness of your 2 x 3's plus two times the thickness of the Jamb Casing material to the finished opening width that you figured. Glue and nail up the Front Wall Frame as you did the Floor Frame. Now use a handsaw to cut the Sill out flush against the Studs as shown. Use the piece cut out as the Door Header. Cut Legs to the finished opening Height that you figured plus the thickness of the Head Casing material and the thickness of the Doorsill material. Glue and nail them in place.

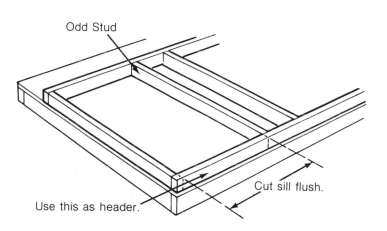

Odd Stud

Use this as header.

Cut sill flush.

4-3 Detail

4-4 Front Wall Panel   Turn
the completed Front Wall
Frame over so the Interior
Surface is uppermost. Cut
the Surfacing material to fit
it as indicated. Nail the Surfacing in place, using the
type of nails recommended
by the manufacturer of the
material you've selected. You
have now finished the Front
Wall Panel.

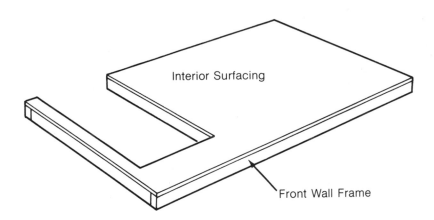

Interior Surfacing

Front Wall Frame

4-4

4-5 Back Wall Panel Make the Back Wall in the same manner. (The Length is the same as that of the Front Frame and you've already figured out the Height.) Because the Access Panel Opening will always be filled with something, it can be wider than the Doorway. If it can be smaller than two feet wide, you will not need the Odd Stud; just work against the regularly spaced Stud as indicated. Cut Header and Legs for the opening the same way you did before. There will be no Head or Jamb Casing or Doorsill, so the actual rough opening size is not critical. Glue and nail the Frame. Then turn it over and install the Interior Surfacing.

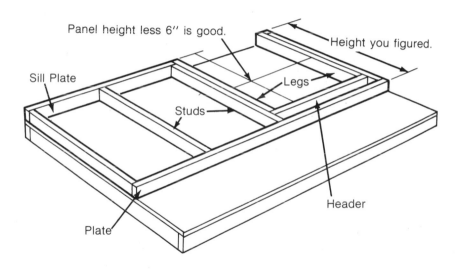

Panel height less 6″ is good.

Height you figured.

Sill Plate

Legs

Studs

Header

Plate

4-5

If you're an accomplished carpenter, you've probably been working outside and have the walls all framed and sheathed. If you're making panels nights in the basement, hoping to finish up Saturday in the yard, read on.

4-6 End Wall Panel This is the tough one. Work on top of the Floor Platform. On the Plywood Floor, mark a line parallel to the front edge of the Floor Platform, in from that edge the thickness of the Front Wall Panel (the width of a 2 x 3 plus the thickness of the Interior Surfacing material). Mark a second line in from the back edge of the Floor Platform the same distance. You will frame the End Walls to fit between these lines. Measure up the Front *Line* the height of the Front Wall Panel. Measure up the Back *Edge* of the Floor Platform the height of the Back Wall Panel. It will be a help to actually draw the line representing the top of the completed End Panel. You'll need one right-hand and one left-hand End Panel, naturally. Cut the End Wall Panel Sill to fit from line to line. Cut the End Wall Panel Plate a bit long so it can be trimmed flush, as shown. Cut the Studs to fit between Sill and Plate, angling the cut for a good fit. You'll need only three Studs if your End Frame is less than 32" wide. Make two such Frames. Cut two pieces of Interior Surfacing and install it on the interior side of each Frame, thus completing the End Panels.

4-6 End Wall Panels

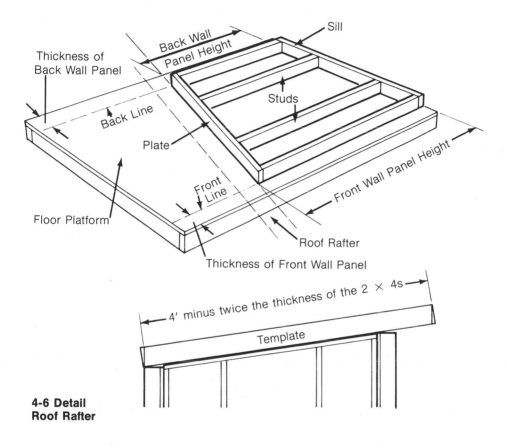

Thickness of Back Wall Panel

Back Wall Panel Height

Sill

Back Line

Studs

Plate

Front Wall Panel Height

Front Line

Floor Platform

Roof Rafter

Thickness of Front Wall Panel

4' minus twice the thickness of the 2 × 4s

Template

**4-6 Detail
Roof Rafter**

While one Panel is still in place on the Floor Platform, use it to aid in marking the Roof Rafters. By sliding a Rafter along the top edge of the Panel, you can mark both ends for cutting so *that* Rafter can act as a Template for the other Rafters.

Note that 4'0" is standard width for most panel materials. Consider it maximum width for the shed-style roof on any house whose Front to Back measurement is between 38" and 44". For a larger house you'll have to piece the Roof Sheathing. For a smaller one you can figure the amount of overhang you'd like when you lay out the Rafter length to mark the angle cut.

4-7 Roof Frame   Although it will be larger than the Floor Platform, frame the Roof Panel on the Floor Platform as you did the Wall Panels. Note that the Ridge Header fits to the *top* of the Rafters while the Eaves Header fits square to the *bottom*. Glue and nail through the Headers into the Rafters.

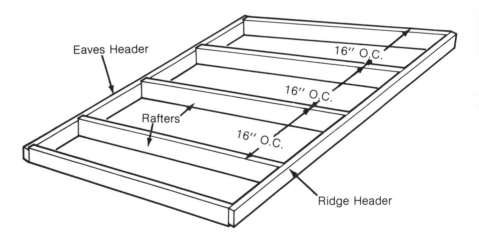

Eaves Header

16" O.C.

16" O.C.

Rafters

16" O.C.

Ridge Header

4-7 Roof Frame

4-8 On the Site   If you haven't decided where to put the doghouse, now is the time. A doghouse this size is not something you pick up and carry from one side of the yard to the other as the wind changes.

Level four concrete blocks or two railroad ties to set it on. Carry or hand-truck the Floor Panel outside and set it on the prepared piers. If it is not going to be level, let the doorway be on the low side. Preferably, the doorway will get the least winter wind and the most sun.

If your dog is small you may be able to build his house on 3 x 4 skids, if you think you will want to move it around much.

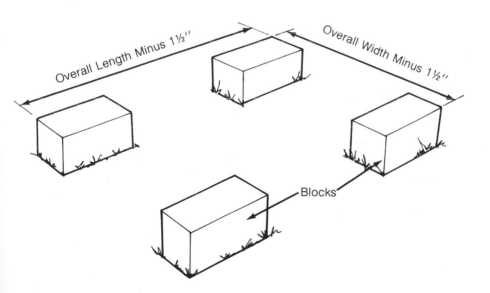

Overall Length Minus 1½''

Overall Width Minus 1½''

Blocks

4-8 On the Site

4-9 Assembly When you're sure you're set, tilt the Front Wall Panel, framed side out, and brace it in place while you nail it fast, flush to the Floor Platform edges as shown. Set, and nail on the End Panels next, then the Back Wall Panel, securing all four panels to each other at the corners as you come to them. Cut and install the Exterior Surfacing on Front and Back Wall Panels, then on the Ends. Now measure and cut Interior Surfacing for the Ceiling. If you are able to get this in one piece, leave it inside the walled-in space. If the doghouse will be too small to work inside of, you can measure for and cut the Ceiling now, but you'll have to install it on the bottom of the Ceiling/ Roof Panel *before* that is set in place.

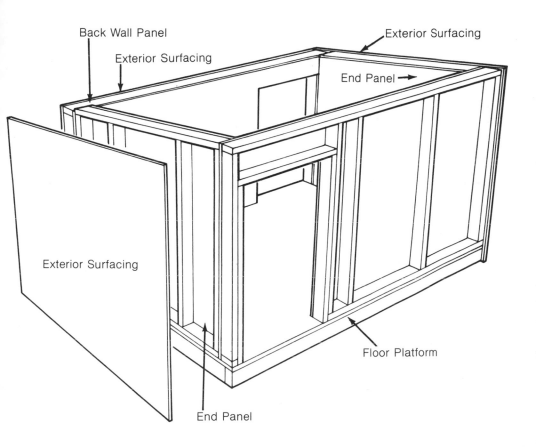

Back Wall Panel

Exterior Surfacing

Exterior Surfacing

End Panel →

Exterior Surfacing

Floor Platform

End Panel

4-9 Assembly

4-10 Roof Assembly Set the Roof Frame in position on top of the Walls. The Eaves Header should be flush with the Exterior Surface of the Back Wall Panel. Scribe and cut the Barge Boards for the ends, then nail them to the outer Rafters. They should overlap the End Wall Panels $3/4''$ to $1\frac{1}{2}''$, and be of a material somewhat thicker than your Cornerboards are. The Barge Boards and Fascias are 1 x 6's on the doghouse shown, with $3/8''$ pine for the Cornerboards. Cut and nail on the Front and Back Fascia Boards next. If you are going to use additional insulation in the roof, install it now, along with the Ceiling. Cutting the Roof Sheathing to fit and nailing it on completes the Roof proper.

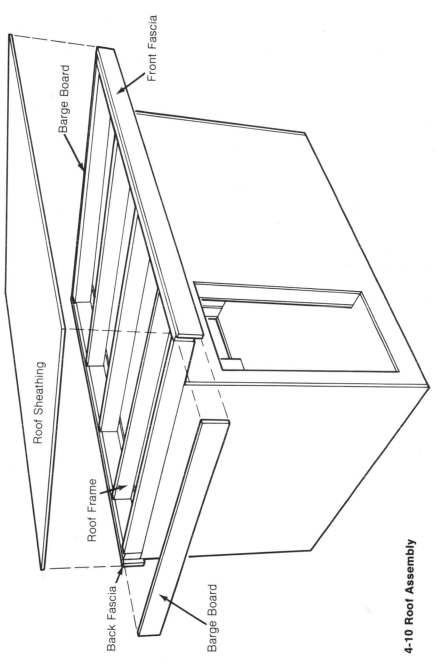

Front Fascia

Barge Board

Roof Sheathing

Roof Frame

Back Fascia

Barge Board

4-10 Roof Assembly

You can group the following tasks under the heading "finishing up" and take your pick of which ones to do first. We dropped our numbering system here because it really doesn't matter if you trim the front Doorway before you install the Access Panel in the rear.

Removable Baffle To make the windbreak or Baffle removable, you will need to mount two angle-shaped strips. (Two 1 x 2's joined as L-shaped units will do nicely for both the Ceiling and Wall Angles—see diagram.) Run one such unit up the Front Wall, fastening through to a Stud and one, notched out as shown, onto the Ceiling. We used a Panel of Homasote®, framed as shown and reinforced up the vulnerable corner with an additional Strip. This bolts to the leg of the Ceiling Angle and, using Staging Nails (double headed), simply pins to the floor. With a little juggling, it can be completely removed for summer.

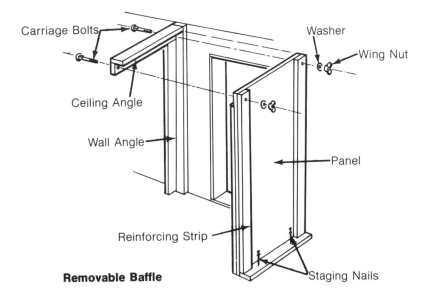

Removable Baffle

Soffit Whether you insulated the roof or not, you still need to close in the space under the overhang. Using a strip of Hardboard cut to fit is an easy way to accomplish this. Hold it in place with a wood Strip fastened to the back of the Front Fascia and another strip fastened through the hardboard, up into each Rafter. If you feel ventilation of the enclosed roof spaces is advantageous, balance two $1\frac{1}{2}''$ diameter regular series Midget Louvers® through the Back Fascia and Eaves Rafter, with two $1''$ diameter LD series Midget Louvers® in each space between Rafters set into the Soffit.

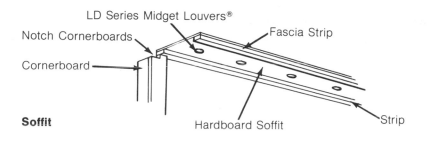

LD Series Midget Louvers®

Notch Cornerboards

Cornerboard

Fascia Strip

Soffit

Hardboard Soffit

Strip

Cornerboards To trim the whole doghouse, we chose to use thin cornerboards of $\frac{3}{8}''$-thick material. Whatever you find readily available that will give the effect you want is suitable. The raw edges of most panel materials require some protection from physical damage and the white-painted accent seems appropriate. The strips at the front will usually require notching to fit under the Barge Boards. Otherwise, it is simply a matter of cutting the Cornerboards to length, painting them, and attaching them in position.

NOTE ON PAINTING   We used the Homasote® with the screened side showing on the Interior of the doghouse, the pebbly side out on the Exterior. Either takes paint readily. Use a good quality primer and, preferably, an acrylic latex (exterior) paint, and seal the edges. The neatest way to paint white trim like this, where it is immediately adjacent to a strong color, is to paint both while they are apart. That is, do the Interior Homasote®, then the Exterior Homasote®. Cut and fit the trim but take it away somewhere to paint it. Then nail it on and just touch up the nailheads.

Doorway   To trim the entrance Doorway, cut Doorsill and Head Casing to the width of the rough Opening. Cut Jamb Casings to fit between Head and Sill. Fit the four strips (We used $\frac{1}{4}$"-thick hardboard) flush with the Exterior Surfacing and let them extend $\frac{1}{2}$" inside. Paint and nail in place. Cut and fit a Flat Frame of molding stock (we used $\frac{3}{4}$" x $1\frac{1}{4}$" strips) as Trim to cover the join between Casing and Surfacing. Paint and nail in place.

Doorway

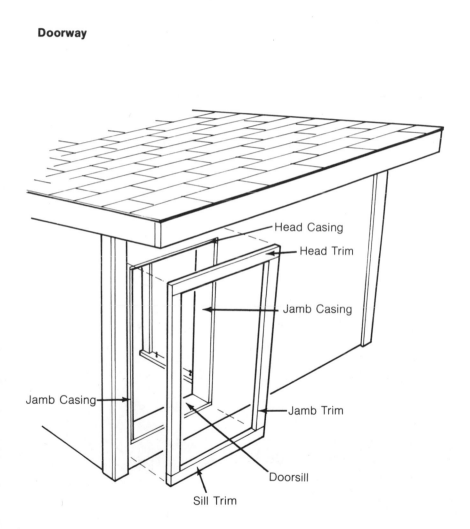

Access Panel Opening   To seat the Access Panel, it is necessary to create a ledge around the top and sides of the rear Opening. We used ³/₄″ x 1³/₄″ Strips (shown from inside the doghouse). Top and Side Strips project into the opening ½″ to ³/₄″. In a smaller house you will want to do this before the roof is on.

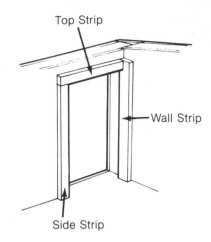

Access Panel Opening

Summer Access Panel   The Summer Access Panel is a similar 2 x 3 Frame-on-Edge sized to fit the Opening and covered with insect Screening stapled in place. A similar Flat Frame of white-painted Trim covers this and fits flush with the Cornerboard and the Jamb Casing Strip and is held in place with the same Turnbuttons.

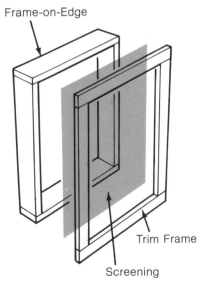

Summer Access Panel

Winter Access Panel   The Winter Access Panel is simply a section of Exterior Wall—a 2 x 3 Frame-on-Edge sized to fit the Opening with a Flat Frame of white-painted Trim on its exterior surface. This Frame fits flush with the Cornerboard and the Jamb Casing Strip shown, where Turnbuttons are installed to hold either Access Panel in place.

Winter Access Panel

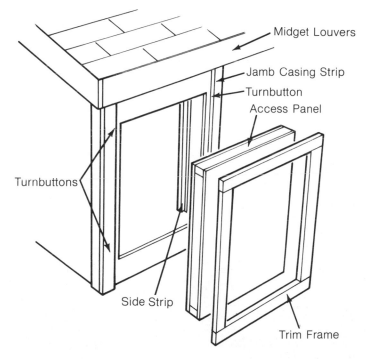

ROOFING This low a pitch on a human-dwelling roof would require that special low-pitch asphalt roofing specifications be followed. On a doghouse, you're probably not going to go to that much trouble. Half-lap roll roofing can be used; stick-down tab shingles are appropriate and durable. Your local building materials supplier can suggest what he has in stock in the small amount that would be needed. Do try to follow the manufacturer's recommendations though as to type and number of nails, etc. Your dog will really appreciate a dry doghouse.

Careful attention to all the small tasks involved in this project will take time. Your dog will appreciate the care you took in making the roof well so he stays dry. The removable Access Panels make cleaning out the doghouse a lot easier. A neat paint job will make the doghouse an attractive addition to your yard, but wait until the paint is dry before you have the dog move in.

CATS

Cats have character and cheek. They'll tell you what they like and don't like by using it or not as their fancy dictates. As it is with all animals, observation of your pet's activities will give you clues about what they might like you to build for them. A general knowledge of cats will tip you off to supply some items that can, with the kitten's cooperation, develop good responses in your new kitten rather than behavior problems.

The cat who lounges on the back of the sofa to see out the window—and you want a new sofa and you don't want him on it—may well be retrained to use a window seat of his own, if you make the window seat before you get the new sofa. The cat that already lounges on the windowsill will appreciate a wider one, and the high ends will save a bit of wear and tear on your draperies. (A smallish dog might like a window seat of his own, too. If he'll fit, why not?) Do take care that an over-excited pet cannot fall out an open window, though.

Think ahead a bit. The cat that goes along on family vacations needs a carrier. You need a carrier for transporting the cat that doesn't want to go to the veterinarian or to be groomed. Sometimes you'll find a willing cat who permits himself to be transported without difficulty. More often a bit of force is needed. Making a combined catbed/carrier ought to help. If the carrier is presented as a bed, and perhaps even used as a bed, the cat won't be awfully apprehensive when you set in the removable door and fasten it closed—at least not the first time. The perforated ends and front will provide plenty of air. (Not if you sandwich it in between two suitcases and the picnic cooler, though. Watch how you pack pets.) The carrier is not meant for use as a shipping container and should not be used that way. On a family vacation, it is a way to bring a bit of home with you for your cat.

If your cat scratches your furniture or knocks over its scratching post, maybe you can train it to scratch a cattree instead. A little catnip tucked under the carpeting might help. If you start with a kitten and punish it regularly for infractions, you may be able to avoid furniture damage entirely, but cats who have not been declawed (and remember that declawing robs them of their natural defenses) need to sharpen and groom their claws. The spartan model gives you a place to hang leash, collar, and comb too. Or you might build the dog shelf for your cat's things instead. Some cats will leap up onto furniture—perhaps you can lure yours to leap up onto his very own furniture if you build the "handyman special" cattree. Others, maybe closer to nature, know that trees are meant to be climbed; these cats show no hesitation in climbing an indoor one you've made for them with whatever special talent you possess. But a cat that doesn't show any inclination to climb won't automatically become a daredevil treetopper just because you installed a cattree. Know your cat.

WINDOW SEAT Project 5

To make a cat window seat that fits your window, the first thing to do is to determine the size of that window. You'll want to know—accurately—the dimension inside the jambs, from stop bead on the left to stop bead on the right. The design we show goes under the bottom sash, preventing it from closing completely. If this bothers you and you own the window sill, you can figure on a permanent installation which will allow the window to open and close behind the window seat. This may also be the solution if you do not have double-hung windows.

5-1 Cut a piece of ½″ plywood to fit comfortably in the space noted, making it 10″ to 12″ wide, depending on the thickness of your window Sash (usually 1⅜″), the width of the window Sill (older ones are usually more generous), and the size of your cat. Cut a Strip of 1 x 2 (or ⅝ x 2 if your Sill is unusually thick) the same length as the Bottom. Glue and nail the Strip along the back edge of the Bottom. Check to see that it fits over the Stool and under the slightly open Sash properly. Measure from the face of the Bottom Sash to the front edge of the plywood Bottom and subtract ¾″. Let that be the width of the window seat Ends.

Double-Hung Window
5-1 Bottom Sash

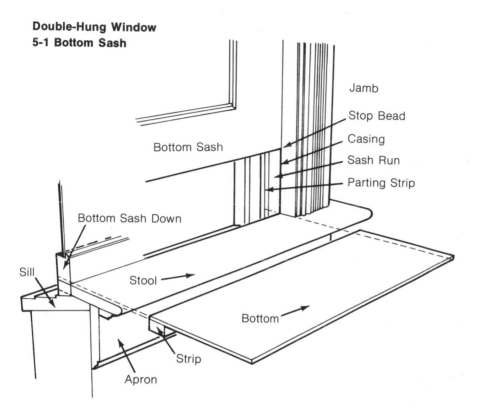

5-2 Make two End Panels as shown, sandwiching Perforated Aluminum between two Flat Frames of 1 x 2's. The overall height of these panels is your choice, depending to some degree on your cat's curtain-raising habits, other furniture near the windows, and the amount of scrap 1 x 2 you have on hand. With a 9″ width, the 12″ height to which the seat shown was built is a good proportion. The easiest way to assemble the Ends is simply to glue one Frame, catch the Aluminum with a few staples, and nail and glue on the opposing Frame, making sure you have the unit flat and square. With soft wood and a heavy hand (use a block if you do have to pound hard), staples and Aluminum will not prevent the two Frames from fitting tightly together, so you won't need to rabbet out for the Aluminum.

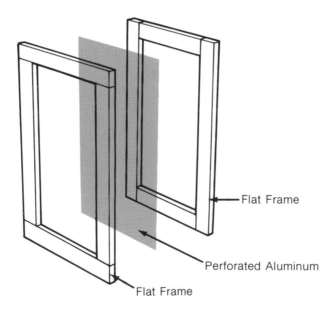

Flat Frame

Perforated Aluminum

Flat Frame

5-2

5-3 If you want to copy the Brackets shown, we've provided this diagram. Each square equals 1″. Enlarge by ruling off 1″ squares, copying the curves square by square. A band saw is ideal for cutting two such Brackets at once, but a coping saw can cope, too. If you design your own Brackets, bear in mind they must clear the Sill and come against the wall below the Apron.

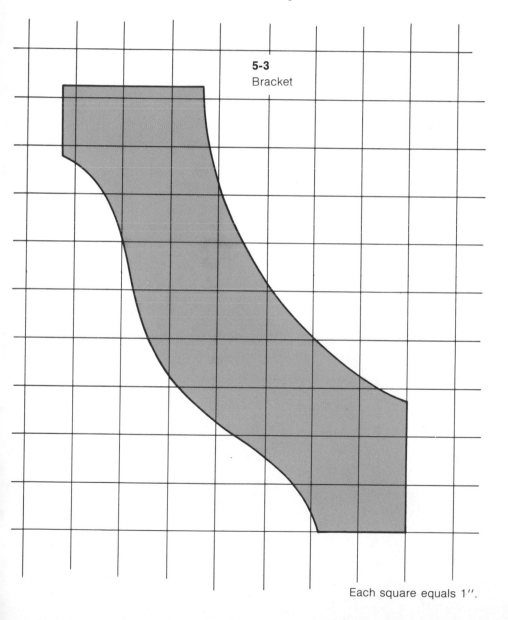

5-3
Bracket

Each square equals 1″.

5-4 To complete the seat, cut a Front piece, the same length as the Bottom, of material about 3″ wide; ⅜″ or ½″ actual thickness is ideal. Cut a Back piece to the same length minus the thickness of both End Panels. Glue and nail through the Bottom into the End Panels, through the End Panels into the Back, and through the Front into the End Panels. Set the window seat in position in the window to locate the Brackets properly. Lower the window. Check with your level and drill as indicated for Screws through Bottom into brackets. It is best to use flat-headed Screws, countersinking the holes, to save your cat from a painful encounter.

5-4

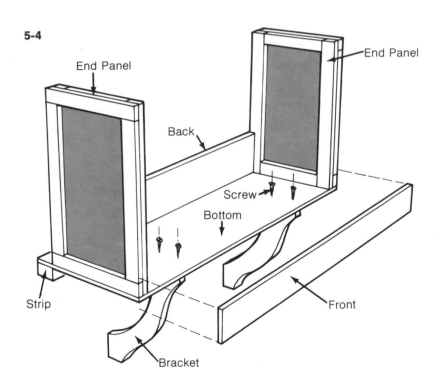

End Panel

End Panel

Back

Screw

Bottom

Strip

Front

Bracket

5-5 For added comfort, you may wish to make a padded seat. The easiest way we found is to cut a piece of 1" or perhaps 2" latex foam to fit snugly into the seat box. With one seam prepare a fabric "sleeve" to fit over it snugly. Fold in both ends as you would in wrapping a package, tucking the raw edges in, under the foam. Sew closed at both ends.

5-5

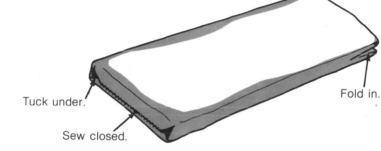

Tuck under.

Sew closed.

Fold in.

Now take it all out of the window and remove the seat pad. Sand down the wood, and give special attention to the aluminum prior to finishing. We suggest light sanding with very fine sandpaper and wiping with lacquer thinner. Use primer and paint recommended for aluminum. When the paint is absolutely dry, put the seat cushion back in, install the works in your cat's favorite window, and put the draperies out of the way beyond the seat ends. Invite your cat to recline. If he's so well trained to keep off furniture that he snubs you, put the pad on the floor until he investigates and sits on it. Then he'll know that not only is it all right, but he's invited to sit on the pad when it is in the windowseat.

BED/CARRIER Project 6

(see also color plate 3)

As is true of most of these projects, size is pretty much up to you and your pet. The cat bed/carrier shown is nominally 12" x 18" x 15" high, ample for four half-grown kittens or one large cat on a long car ride. A resident cat whose preferences you know probably has a favorite box or basket, the size of which can guide you in arriving at some figures. Be generous if you antici- pate long trips, and take along a leash and collar or harness so you can walk your cat safely at frequent rest stops along the way.

If you use the anodized perforated aluminum, as we did, and want to preserve the gold color unbesmirched by walnut stain, alter the assembly order a bit. Cut and assemble everything *except* the aluminum and the decorative frame as indicated. Remember to stain enough molding to make the frames when you are staining the wooden parts after you have panels, front, and bottom joined together. Do the handle and the door flat frame at the same time, of course. When the stain is dry, cut and nail on the four decorative frames to hold the unsullied gold aluminum in place. This kind of think-ahead planning is suggested whenever you have dissimilar materials and want to finish only some of them.

6-1 You'll need a piece of ½″ plywood for the Bottom, cut to whatever size you have determined will do. Make two End Panels, as shown, sandwiching perforated aluminum between a Flat Frame and a lighter Decorative Frame. The bed/carrier shown uses a Flat Frame of stock that measures $^{11}/_{16}″$ x $1^{5}/_{16}″$ (actual dimensions), which you can get by ripping 1 x 3's down the center. The mitered Decorative Frame is made of screen molding, ¼″ x ¾″. Whatever you find close to those sizes will do splendidly. And if you don't have a miter box, do not despair. Butt Jointed Decorative Frames hold the Aluminum on just as well.

Make the heavier Flat Frame the same width as the Bottom and however high you have determined is proper for your cat. Align the *inside* dimensions of the Decorative Frame with the *inside* dimensions of the Flat Frame. Hardboard ⅛″ thick is probably easiest to use for the Back. Make the width equal to the Bottom dimension plus two times the thickness of the Flat Frame material. The height of the Back is the same as the height of the Flat Frame. Cut a Back Strip of 1 x 1 to fit between the Flat Frames and glue and nail it along the top edge of the Back, making it flush with the top edge.

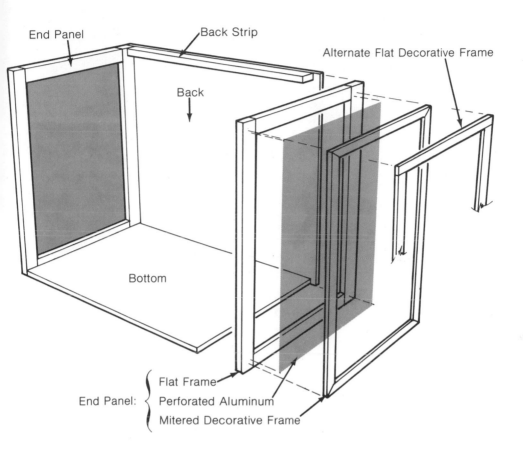

End Panel

Back Strip

Alternate Flat Decorative Frame

Back

Bottom

End Panel:
{
Flat Frame
Perforated Aluminum
Mitered Decorative Frame

6-1

6-2 The Door and Front are both the same length as the Bottom. Make up a Door and a Front in the same manner as you made the End Panels, but plan it so that the Rabbeted Joint, closed, gives you a Total Height of Door plus Front plus the thickness of the plywood Bottom equal to the height of the End Panels. If you have no means of making the rabbet cut, a thin strip of wood, glued and nailed on the back of the Door's Flat Frame to project down, coming behind the top of the Front, will do almost as well.

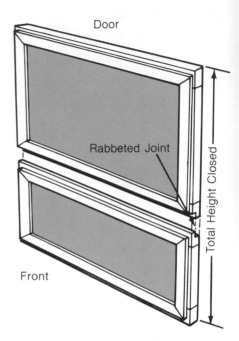

6-2

6-3 To duplicate the Handle shown you will need a piece of 1″ stock 10½″ long by 2½″ wide. Enlarge the diagram so each square is 1″ x 1″ and copy the outline square by square. If you'll fold your Pattern on the Centerline indicated, cut on the enlarged outline, and unfold it, you'll have a reasonably good template for the whole Handle outline. If you make a shorter carrier, you will probably want a shorter handle. Don't cut the finger room under 4″, however; this means you could safely make the overall Handle length 8½″ with this same outline by eliminating two squares (or one square from the half pattern) at the centerline.

6-3

Each square equals 1″.

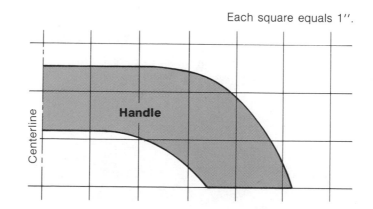

Centerline

Handle

6-4 You'll need to cut a Top piece (⅛"-thick hardboard is fine) with a width equal to the width of the End Panel plus the thickness of the Back and a length the same as the length of the Back. Use screws and glue to attach the Handle in the center of the Top. Glue and nail through Bottom into Front, glue and nail End Panels to Bottom and Front, and glue and nail on Back. Cut Keeper strips and, with Door in place, check their location before gluing and nailing them inside End Panels as shown. (If you did not Rabbet the Joint between Front and Door, Keeper must be cut shorter to permit the Door with added strip to be set in place properly.) Get Door out of the way while you glue and nail through Top, into End Panels and Back Strip. Set the Door in position and drill through Top and into Door for the two Pins. A ⅛" Dowel with a wooden Bead glued onto it makes an easily operated closing Pin. If you think you'll lose them, glue each end of a string under a bead and wrap it around the handle, or thread it through the perforated Door.

6-5 Finish it off with a puffy pillow made the simple way. Measure out two rectangles of Fabric slightly larger than the Bottom (allow ⅝" for seam all around). Seam around, leaving a hole at one end through which to insert stuffing. Stuff with dacron or polyester fiber, shredded latex, or whatever suits your cat. Sew the opening closed. Call the cat. Let him think it is a bed first, closing him in with the removable Door only when you need to.

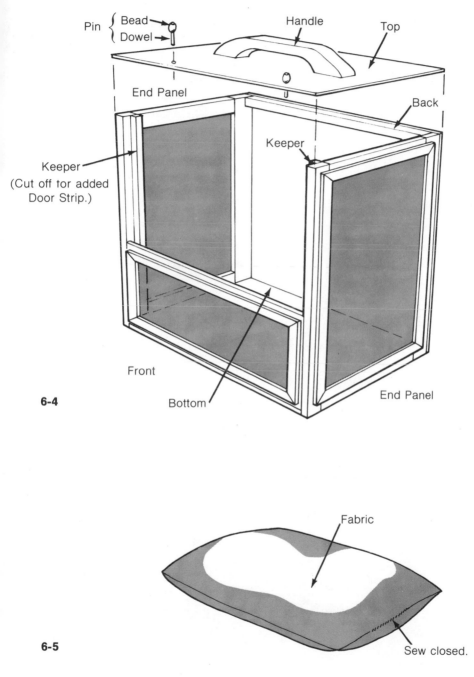

Pin { Bead
     { Dowel

Handle

Top

End Panel

Back

Keeper

Keeper
(Cut off tor added
Door Strip.)

Front

Bottom

End Panel

6-4

Fabric

Sew closed.

6-5

LUMBER CATTREES Project 7

For the cat who has everything else, for the handyman or woman who isn't, very, here's a project idea that will wake up your imagination, to say nothing of your cat's. Once you know there is a springloading device (called a Timber-Topper℠), made in two styles, easily available by mail order if you can't find it locally, your imagination just may run away with you. In the first group of projects using Timber-Toppers℠ you'll find an easy way to install floor-to-ceiling scratching posts. In the second group we show how even an apartment-dwelling cat can have his very own tree to climb.

For the lumber cattrees you will need a No. 50 Timber-Topper℠, a standard 2 x 3 cut a few inches shorter than the distance between your floor and your ceiling, some carpet scraps, and carpet tacks. Cut the 2 x 3 as instructed on the Timber-Topper℠ device. For the "Spartan Model" that's all you'll need. For the "Handyman Special" you will also need some ½″-thick plywood scrap pieces. Either way, tack the Carpet around it, starting just above the Floor and going up as high as your cat can stretch. Set the springloading device on the top end of the 2 x 3. Position it on the ceiling. Lift the 2 x 3 and compress the spring until you have the 2 x 3 in True Vertical Position and can let it spring back against the floor. (See following page.) Presto—a floor-to-ceiling scratching post your cat can't tip over.

If he's not a climber, it's safe to install a couple of cup hooks or accessory hooks for a place to hang up the leash if he has one, and a brush and comb. If he does climb, don't do this. A climbing cat with a collar could get hung up—and hanged—on the hooks.

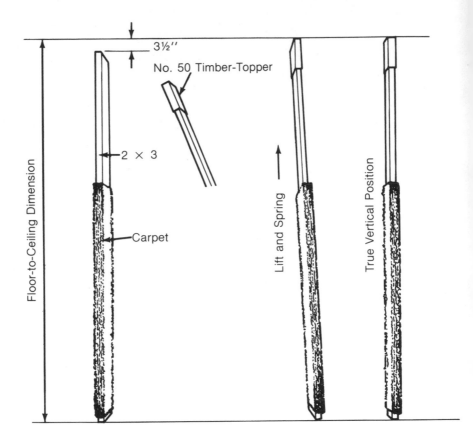

3½''

No. 50 Timber-Topper

Floor-to-Ceiling Dimension

2 × 3

Carpet

Lift and Spring

True Vertical Position

Spartan Model

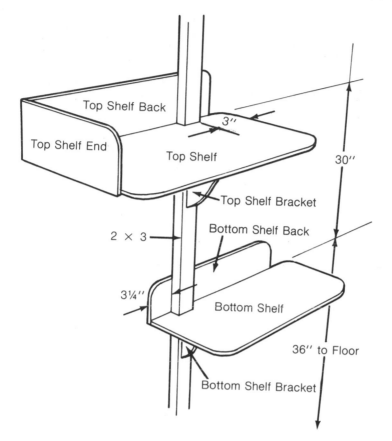

Handyman Special Assembly

To duplicate the "Handyman Special" we worked out for a couple of furniture-jumping feline gymnasts, you'll need ½"-thick plywood scraps in the following sizes:

Bottom Shelf	10" x 20"
Bottom Shelf Back	17½" x 4¾"
Top Shelf	14" x 21"
Top Shelf Back	19½" x 6"
Top Shelf End	12½" x 6"

Notch both Shelves as shown for the 2 x 3, which needs to be $3\frac{1}{2}''$ shorter than your Floor-to-Ceiling Dimension. Cut the two Brackets from 1″ stock according to the square grid pattern provided, enlarging each square to 1″ x 1″.

Glue and nail through Shelf Back into Shelf. Glue and nail through Top Shelf End into Top Shelf and Top Shelf Back. Glue and nail Top Shelf to the 2 x 3 66″ up from floor; set in Top Bracket, gluing and nailing it in place. Glue and nail Bottom Shelf to the 2 x 3 36″ up from floor and glue and nail Bottom Bracket under it. There is no magic in the exact sizes given. Just make the shelves large enough for a cat to land on. They do seem to prefer a backstop of

Each square equals 1″.

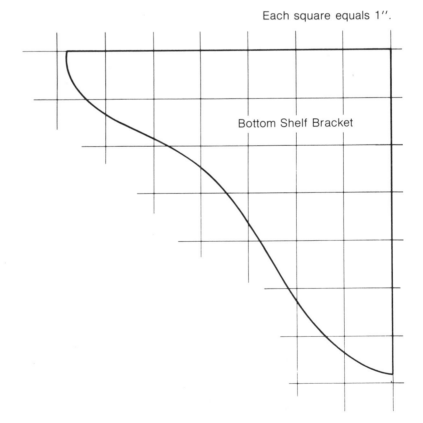

Bottom Shelf Bracket

Your dog will be warm and dry in the doghouse, shown here
painted barn red. (Project begins on page 50.)

The deck and outdoor water dish provide a perfect setting for a restful afternoon in the sun. (Deck begins on page 42; water dish begins on page 39.)

Your cat—or kittens—can travel comfortably and sleep soundly in this bed/carrier. (Project begins on page 84.)

Keep your gerbils happy with a toy like this gym. Their antics will delight you. (Project begins on page 180.)

Above: The guinea pig cage is shown here with the bungalow and tunnel toy. (Cage begins on page 148; bungalow begins on page 156; tunnel toy begins on page 159.) Below: As your guinea pig's curiosity leads him from bungalow to tunnel, you can admire his charm and your handiwork.

A natural cattree—the Macrame Model is shown here—can be a playground for your cat and a visual treat for you. (Project begins on page 106.)

Above: Give your birds a chance to spread their wings in this flight cage. (Project begins on page 112.) Below: The birds in this closeup are secure on their perch in their decorative and spacious flight cage. (Project begins on page 120.)

Above: The vivarium and cabinet provide room for your pet and for pet-care accessories. (Project begins on page 132.) Below: The anole shown here is luxuriating in the miniature woodland built into the viarium.

some sort. Tack Carpet around lower part of 2 x 3. Slit and turn raw edges under where it encounters Bottom Bracket. A second piece of Carpet can be affixed around the 2 x 3 between Shelves, too. Using a No. 50 Timber-Topper®, repeat the installation procedure, the same as for the "Spartan Model."

Each square equals 1″

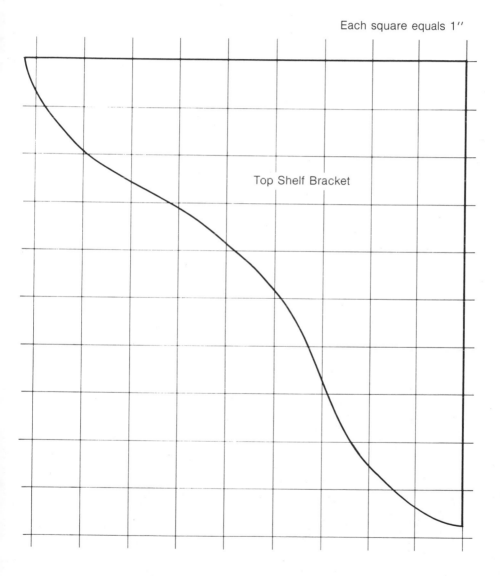

Top Shelf Bracket

NATURAL CATTREES Project 8

(see also color plate 7)

The next three cattrees are what we call "the naturals" because all three use real tree branches cut to length and whittled down to approximate the 1⅝" diameter that the No. 52 wooden Timber-Topper® accommodates. It works on the same principle as the metal one but is meant for a standard closet pole—which you can use if you cannot locate suitable branches. For branches, try your local tree service, follow the phone- or light-company tree-trimming crews, or just look around after a good windstorm. You want a "tree" that's not too springy and has one relatively straight section that's slightly over 8' long. Try to get a branch whose smaller branches are also intact and are as long as possible. That way, you have the best chance to trim it to suit your taste and your craft medium.

These are, obviously, one-of-a-kind designs, not meant to be copied exactly. The first one may appeal to the woodworking grown-up who never had a tree house. The cats we've tested really seemed to enjoy the slight movement that comes naturally in the two cord-strung models, one using macrame techniques, the other based on twined basketry. If you'd rather sew, there's no reason a sling-seat of strong fabric won't work.

Your cat will probably have to be shown how to climb into his new perch, but once there, he'll love it. And you'll have a conversation piece like no other. We offer a few hints to get you moving. They won't make a climber out of a scaredy-cat, but if your cat enjoys high seclusion, try one of these projects.

The "Tree-House Model" consists of a $\frac{1}{2}''$-thick plywood platform supported by two 1 x 2 cleats nailed onto the branches. A triangular arrangement of forking branches is best, simply because it is most stable. Try to get the platform set so it will be fairly level when the tree is sprung into position with a No. 52 Timber-Topper™.

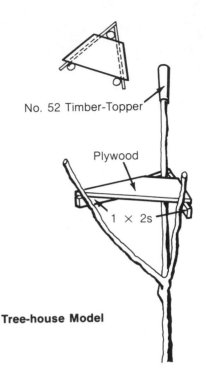

No. 52 Timber-Topper

Plywood

1 × 2s

Tree-house Model

For the "Basketry Natural," three-point suspension is also best. If you make baskets at all, you'll recognize that the twining method, using glazed venetian blind cord and leaving the Spokes extra long, is the basis of this design. The "platter" was ended off with a three-rod coil, braiding the Weaver ends and letting them drop to a wrapped tassel. Three groups of Spoke strands were collected and knotted about the branches as shown, bent down and wrapped to secure the ends. The remaining ones were worked off in a standard reed basketry border and allowed to fall free. We glued all the knots.

Again, the cattree is installed using a No. 52 Timber-Topper℗.

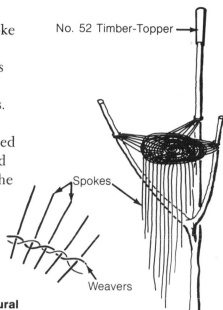

No. 52 Timber-Topper →

Spokes

Weavers

Basketry Natural

Macrame is extremely versatile, and once you see how a triangular shape can be established, all else comes easily. With only one branch branching at the right level, we made the opposite side of a triangle in this cattree by hanging a Stick from two higher points like a trapeze, as shown at A. Tensioning Suspenders and Guys keeps it in place. Starting strands were lark's-headed over the upright branches and tied off with clove hitches at the "fringe" ends. A pattern of Alternating Square Knots in alternating directions was used throughout. The material again is glazed venetian blind cord. If macrame is your medium, go to it. An alternate approach to establishing a triangle with two rigid sides is shown at B. Naturally, you can also work a circular piece and tie it in place the same way the basketry version was done. Mount the finished cattree using a No. 52 Timber-Topper®.

Any of these approaches can work in stitched fabric as well. Just pick your technique, understand the problem, and solve it your way.

Let your cat show you how he solves the problem of getting into the cattree perch. Put him there first, if he's a slow learner. You may also have to show him how to get down. Younger cats are likely to have fewer inhibitions about this cattree; your older cat may like it once he's up there but may never learn to get up and down without your help.

Macrame Model

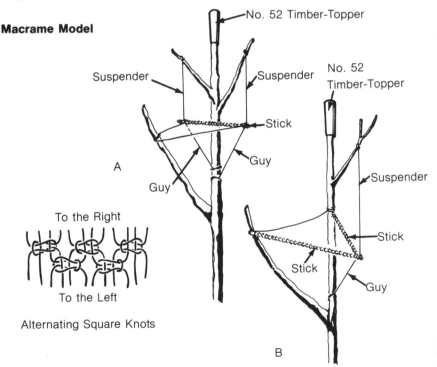

A

To the Right

To the Left

Alternating Square Knots

No. 52 Timber-Topper

Suspender

Suspender

No. 52 Timber-Topper

Stick

Guy

Guy

Suspender

Stick

Stick

Guy

B

BIRDS

Some birds have only the tiny cage they are accustomed to sleeping in. They'll chirp and tweet merrily away and you'll let them out to play, allowing them to have free run of the house. The poor dears promptly singe their feathers going too close to the stove, scald themselves seeking a shower under the hot water faucet, or, worse yet, escape through the open window. A safer bet is a flight cage.

FLIGHT CAGE Project 9

(see also color plates 8 and 9)

We've made our design decorative enough so that it no longer needs to be kept in the kitchen—which isn't the best room in the house for birds anyway because of its temperature and humidity variations.

Making the Cage Back of hardboard gives you a place to be creative and relate the cage to your decor. We used artist's acrylic paints, then sprayed the work with non-toxic clear varnish. The mirror strip in our cage is a scrap of plastic; a mirror is certainly not a necessity, though some birds do enjoy watching themselves perform.

Birds need perches, but there is no rule that says the perches must be the full width of the cage. In this design, the whole dowel Perch Tree comes out for cleaning. There's a door halfway up the cage side on the right for access to the birds, and one at the bottom on the left for cleaning the cage and removing litter. Use cedar cage carpets cut to fit the cage bottom. It is safest to put in a good pad of newspaper on a piece of plastic or aluminum foil first, then the carpet. Roll the pad and carpet together for removal. Easily cleaned, the colorful acrylic plastic Feeder with water and seed compartments should be washed out once a day.

You can hang the flight cage by chains, as shown in the black-and-white photograph, or you can set it on its own table like the one shown for the rodent cages.

You could make a flight cage of a design similar to this from 1 x 2's, lattice strip, and woven wire mesh, but you may want something a bit more decorative. Check your lumber and price alternatives. You should find screen stock or other S4S stock (that is stock sanded on all four sides) of sizes suitable for a lighter-looking cage that weighs much less than 1 x 2's would and will take a nicer finish.

9-1 To duplicate the cage shown, you'll need a Top and a Bottom of ½″-thick plywood, two End Frames of ¾″ x 1¼″ screen stock, and a Front Frame using ¾″ x 1¼″ stock for the horizontal pieces and ¾″ x 2″ stock for the uprights. Set in ¾″ x 1¼″ Cross Pieces as shown to form the Door openings. You'll want the Bird Door about mid-height of the cage, large enough to get an arm in and the bird out. The Cleaning Door must be big enough to take out the Perch Tree (rotate it) and to roll up and remove the cage litter. It also has to be high enough so the filled Feeder can be put in right

side up. Glue and nail the End Frames to the Top and Bottom and the Front Frame to End Frames, Top, and Bottom, forming a cage framework one foot deep, two feet wide, and three feet high. Also glue the Frames for the two doors, using ¾″ x 1¼″ stock, making them fit easily into the openings you formed in the End Frames. Wipe up any excess glue before it dries, while it is still wipeable. When the glue is dry, sand the assemblies smooth and ready them for finishing, so you can do all the painting at once. (We sprayed on two coats of non-toxic black satin enamel.)

9-2 Rabbet enough pieces of ½″ x ¾″ screen stock (according to the detail shown) for the Decorative Mitered Frames and paint that material now, too. If you have no easy means of cutting this rabbet, check your lumber yard for trim profiles that could be combined to cover the raw edge of the Expanded Aluminum easily and attractively.

9-2 Section

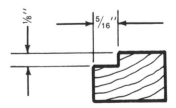

9-1

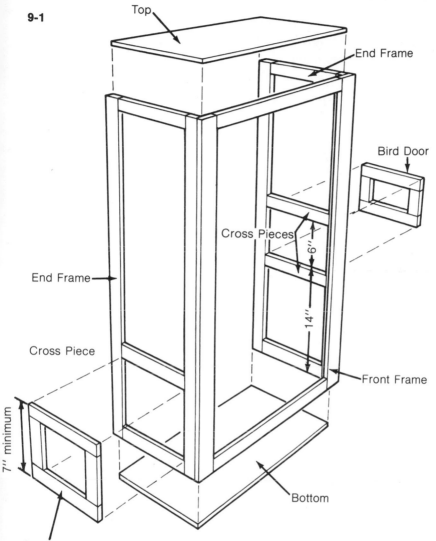

Top

End Frame

Bird Door

Cross Pieces

6''

End Frame

14''

Cross Piece

Front Frame

7'' minimum

Bottom

Cleaning Door

9-3 When the paint is dry, measure each frame opening,. including the openings in each Door, and cut pieces of the Expanded Aluminum ½″ larger in length and width. (We used Gold Vista Decorative Panels.) Take care that you run them in the same direction all the time. You'll find the Do-It-Yourself® Aluminum cuts easily with most kitchen shears. Using staples sparingly, attach each piece to cover each opening indicated, letting the metal overlap the wood ¼″ all around. Cut the rabbeted screen stock to form Mitered Frames around each opening, covering the raw edges of the Expanded Aluminum.. Align inner edges of the Mitered Frames with the inner edges of the Frame and Door Frame openings. Drill the Top for the chain Loops and the Perch Hanger Bolt. (We used the Lamparts® Loops and their Brass Finish Gothic Swag-Lite Chain.) Install the Loops now, using a washer and lock nut on the underside of the Top. You won't be able to reach comfortably to do it later.

9-3 Detail

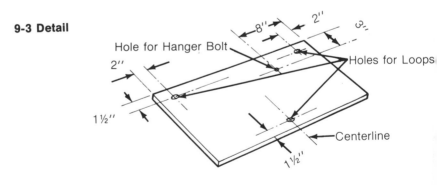

9-3

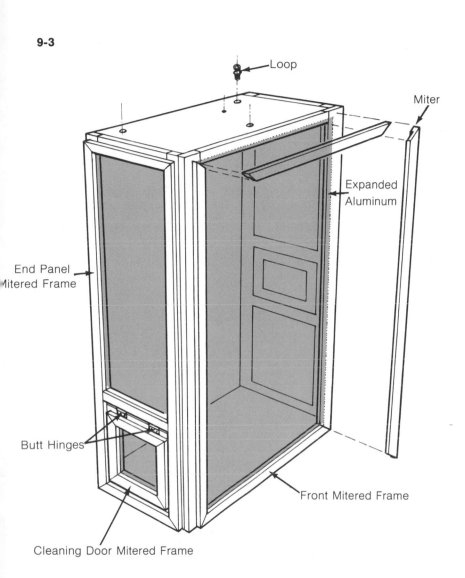

Loop

Miter

Expanded
Aluminum

End Panel
Mitered Frame

Butt Hinges

Front Mitered Frame

Cleaning Door Mitered Frame

9-3 Detail Both Doors are built in the same manner. You will probably find you have to plane a bit off the opening edge of both Doors to make them operate easily. The Cleaning Door is hinged at the top and must be lifted up for access to cage carpets, Feeder, etc. We've latched it simply, drilling through the Door and into the Frame for a bent wire bolt. The Bird Door, shown in this detail view, is hinged at the bottom and falls open when the black (to match the cage) plastic latch is lifted. The latch is 1″ wide by 2½″ long, with the ends rounded. It pivots on a round-headed wood screw driven in snug

9-3 Detail

Latch

Bird Door
Mitered
Frame

Expanded
Aluminum

Butt Hinges

but not too tight. If you have no plastic scraps, use hardboard painted black. The hinges we used on both Doors are 1″ x 1″ brass Butt Hinges. Look for "small box hardware" in your mail order catalogs if you can't find hinges this small locally.

9-4 Using a piece of ⅛″-thick tempered hardboard for the Back gives you a good area to decorate as you wish. Just make sure the finish you use will not harm the future occupants of your flight cage. You'll get a neater joint if you mask the edge margin of the hardboard where it will be covered by the edges of Top, Bottom, and End Panels. The masking tape can be pulled off when you're through painting. We glued on a mirror of scrap plastic,

9-4

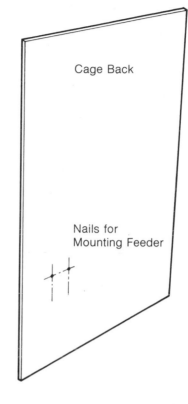

Cage Back

Nails for
Mounting Feeder

but don't be surprised if your birds fly into it when they first tour their cage. If you are making the Cage Feeder, use the drilled Feeder Back Plate as a template for marking the Mounting Nail positions on the cage Back. Drive two Nails in as shown, leaving the heads to project above the surface of the hardboard an amount equal to the thickness of the Feeder Back Plate. Cut off the projecting points and, supporting the heads on a piece of metal, peen over the cut-off ends, holding them in place. (This simply means to mash down straight on the cut-off nails, mushrooming the metal into the back of the hardboard piece.) It is easier to install the Perch Tree now too, before the Back goes on, though the Doors are large enough that you can remove, clean, and replace it from the completed cage. When you are all ready, the Cage Back can be glued and nailed in place. If you used tempered hardboard, drill holes first for the nails.

PERCH TREE  Project 10

(see also color plates 8 and 9)

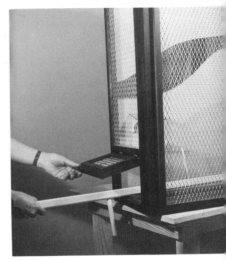

10-1 The Perch Tree may be the simplest project in this book. You'll need a piece of $1\frac{5}{16}''$ x $1\frac{5}{16}''$ S4S square stock 33″ long. Round the corners off well. Drill as indicated for a $\frac{3}{8}''$-diameter Dowel, a $\frac{1}{2}''$-diameter Dowel, and a $\frac{5}{8}''$-diameter Dowel. Cut the Dowels so that $5\frac{1}{2}''$ to 6″ projects. Try to get good hardwood Dowels and don't paint them. To install the Perch Tree, run the wood-threaded end of a $\frac{1}{4}''$ or smaller diameter Hanger Bolt into the top end of the Tree. Let the machine-threaded portion project through the Cage Top. (You drilled the Hole in 9-3.) Secure it with Washer and Wing Nut to permit easy removal and replacement for cleaning.

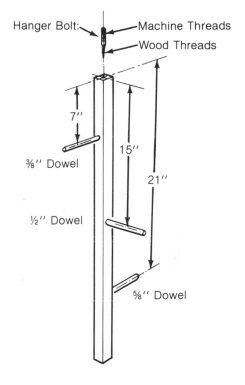

Hanger Bolt: — Machine Threads — Wood Threads

7″

15″

21″

⅜″ Dowel

½″ Dowel

⅝″ Dowel

10-1

CAGE FEEDER Project 11

(see also color plate 8)

11-1 This Cage Feeder is the first of a number of projects to be made of ⅛″-thick acrylic sheet, and in many ways it is the most difficult. If you've never worked with acrylic before, now is a good time to reread the special section on acrylic in chapter 1.

Patterns for all the non-rectangular parts are shown full size here, and the colors we used are noted. You will also need to cut rectangular pieces as listed, plus a length of ⅜″-diameter solid rod for the Perch.

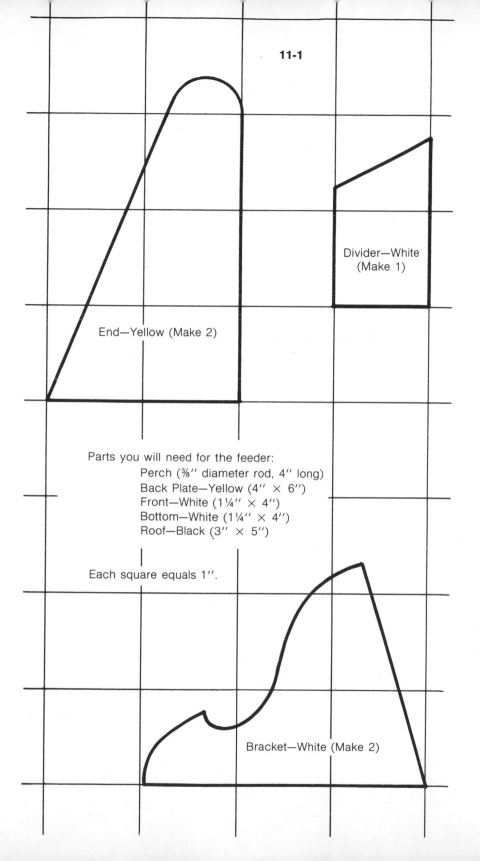

Divider—White
(Make 1)

End—Yellow (Make 2)

Parts you will need for the feeder:
        Perch (⅜" diameter rod, 4" long)
        Back Plate—Yellow (4" × 6")
        Front—White (1¼" × 4")
        Bottom—White (1¼" × 4")
        Roof—Black (3" × 5")

Each square equals 1".

Bracket—White (Make 2)

11-2 To assemble the Feeder, start with the trough part. File and sand the front edge of the Bottom piece to fit snugly against the sloping Front. The Divider governs this angle and should also be sanded. Tape these three pieces together and, using the solvent adhesive, run the glue joints. Cut the Perch rod to 4″, the same length as the Feeder Back Plate. Set the Perch between the Ends, holding them apart with the 4″-long trough assembly. Tape and glue Perch to Ends. Drill the Holes for Keyhole Mounting in the Feeder Back Plate. (Make the two large Holes to clear the nailhead size you will use. The slot must allow the body of the nail to fit there.) Now lay the Feeder Back Plate down flat, set the Ends with the Perch attached to them in place, and locate the trough carefully, taping these parts in place. Glue that much together.

Tape the two Brackets to the Back Plate and the Roof to Back Plate and Brackets and run glue in those joints. Check that the water compartment doesn't leak. (Reglue it if it does.) Sand off any really sharp corners, fill water and seed compartments, and, holding the Cleaning Door of the cage open, put Feeder over nailheads and drop it into place.

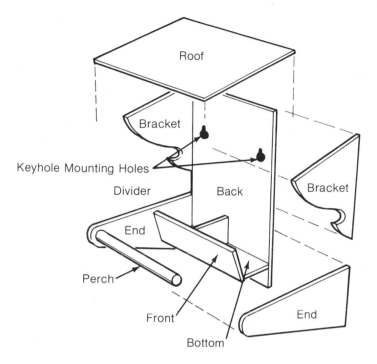

Roof

Bracket

Keyhole Mounting Holes

Divider Back Bracket

End

Perch

Front End

Bottom

11-2 Feeder Assembly

Latch that Door and open the Bird Door. Install the birds. Latch the Bird Door closed and see how long it takes them to find out that the mirror is not an open way out. Once they settle in, they should enjoy their decorative cage. You can hang it from three swag hooks, safe from your other pets, or bring all three chains together for a one-point hanger, though that will spin. The spinning makes some birds dizzy; others don't seem to mind. Remember, though, that you lose control of positioning the cage for the best draft and sun exposures if you hang it from one point.

UNPETTABLE PETS

Probably the least understood group of pets are the sit-and-look-at types for whom you must create an entire environment—land-based for some, aquatic for others, a little bit of both for the amphibians. Although this section might seem to fall naturally into two parts—the case and the cabinet—the two projects are best considered together first. There are two creatures involved in the sitting, too, the sitter and the sittee as it were. Both require consideration.

The implication is obvious. You are going to build something for your pet to sit in comfortably while you sit and watch him. Aquarium or terrarium, you'll want a transparent container of some sort: a vivarium that enables you to observe the activities of your unpettable pet in his natural setting. And that requires something convenient, workable, and attractive to set it on.

Building a waterproof aquarium in the home workshop so well that it doesn't leak 10 or 20 gallons of water onto the ceiling of the room below takes a bit of doing. Store-bought tanks are inexpensive enough to make building your own impractical. The activities of fish in an aquarium can be fascinating, though some species are very demanding. They want the water temperature, the alkalinity, water movement, and lighting all just so. Their feeding arrangements also are apt to require particular attention. You'll want suitable plants and a scavenger population to help you maintain the conditions your marine pets like best. Using a painted hardboard panel behind the tank, tight up against the glass, works well. You can paint a scene on this or just make it a nice color, to provide a background against which your particular fish will show up well. The mechanical means of keeping the water clean and fresh for them can be placed behind the hardboard for a much more attractive installation.

You still need a place to set the tank. The cabinet we include here is designed to be adaptable. A 10-gallon tank is an average-size home aquarium for many fish varieties. It runs about 12″ high, 20″ long, and 10½″ from front to back and, full of fish and water, weighs about the same as a hefty full-grown man. Measure the tank you want to accomodate. The cabinet shown will support the weight. Make sure you have it nicely level before you fill up the aquarium.

A terrarium is something else again. An enclosure for a land-based animal can be built in a home shop. The first thing you need to do is determine the species you intend to house. A pet store specializing in vivarium inhabitants can show you a large variety of frogs, toads, geckoes, iguanas, salamanders, newts, and anoles such as we show, as well as tortoises, turtles, and maybe tadpoles. You might check out likely candidates in your encyclopedia or at your library, too. You won't even know how to size your vivarium case until you decide whether it should be higher than it is deep for your vertically oriented tree-climbing gecko or broad and squat for your slow-moving basically horizontal turtle. Learn a bit about the animal you intend to make a home for before you start construction.

The food requirements of your unpettable pet need consideration too. Maybe you'll find yourself in the cricket-raising business on the side. Some lizards are vegetarians and will learn to like lettuce if more exotic greenery is in short supply, but insect-eaters usually want their lunch alive. A number of reference books in this field give instructions for raising meal-worms, but meal-worms are not the ideal food for many species, according to current authorities. It's best to check with your pet dealer to see what the animal you buy is used to eating.

How you furnish your terrarium/vivarium will depend on the animal it is to house. Nocturnal animals need a shady place to hide when the light is too much for them. Other species like a flat rock for sunning, some want tree branches for climbing, and some like leaves for lounging. Woodland or desert, marsh or bog dweller, each requires plants and materials common to his home territory. None of your pets grew up in a bare plastic box, which is what you have to start with. Once you've determined the size and built the case, you'll need to take it from there according to what inhabitant you selected to be your star sit-and-look-at pet. Plan ahead.

Supplying the enclosure is one thing. Making it work is another. Sunshine lovers require a substitute sun. You may choose a pet that requires dry, hot air, while others like it much more humid. You will need a thermometer and perhaps a heater or maybe a fan or blower to circulate that just-right air. How much and what kind of water your land dwellers require is critical. Some can lap the dew off leaves (you need a mister and a place for stored water to settle out the chlorine), while others require running, filtered water. In between are those happy with water that bubbles a bit. Water in nature is always moving and many of the unpettable pets don't know it is water if it just sits there. Some want an occasional swim, too, but amphibians are probably better off in an aquarium with a little land around the edges.

Settle the water issue first. Water that just sits there gets dirty fast. Water that sits there and bubbles a bit to make it move requires an air pump and an airstone. (The pump forces air through plastic tubing to the stone set in the water where it disperses in bubbles.) Either way, you need to be able to remove the water container easily for cleaning. Water that runs requires a pump and most likely a filter; both are used in aquariums. (The pump lifts the water into the pool while gravity syphons it out.) Somewhere in the circuit a filter is a good idea. We used a combination pump/filter with plastic tubing run through the back wall of the terrarium. Our pool is a three-quart glass bowl. The water is syphoned from the bowl to the filter reservoir and then pumped up to the top of the waterfall where it trickles back to the bowl. You have to have the water at the same level in the reservoir and in the pool when the pump is off. When the pump starts, water is drawn from the reservoir, lowering the level there enough to cause syphon action from pool to filter to commence. Therefore, if you plan running, filtered water, figure out the mechanics first. The depth of your pool and the vertical location of the pump/filter are critical.

Once the pump/filter location is determined and the pool container is set, the general approach to making a terrarium usually starts with blocking in the major land contour with pieces of plastic foam cut to fit. The foam is covered with washed aquarium gravel mixed with activated charcoal (sold as filter charcoal in aquarium supply stores). Next you'll need a layer of potting soil for planting your plants, or clean sand and a dried branch for a true desert dweller. You'll want more specific information than we can give here on selecting the right plants, soil, et cetera, to make your pet feel at home. Ask your pet dealer and your librarian to help you. You should be warned. There are some vegetarian pets that will eat up some of your plants. You might turn out to be running a tree farm for your turtle.

All this has to be maintained. You'll have to clean a pond occasionally, prune and replant foliage every so often, and perhaps remove endangered young of whatever species you have. (Some types can't tell their own young from food and cannibalize indiscriminately.) Unless you have a resident scavenger animal, you are apt to need to do a bit of garbage removal, too. Uneaten food can get pretty smelly. How you make a lid for the case will depend on what, specifically, that lid must do. For our anoles, the requirements were to keep the anoles in and other pets out, let in air and light, be easily lifted to toss in a cricket or two, be completely removable for major work within the terrarium, and be attractive. What access you are going to require will determine whether you need a one-piece lift-off lid, as shown, or a latchable trapdoor in a more stationary cover. What you'll be putting in and taking out of the case will determine the size of the trapdoor.

Once you've considered the matter of tank with lid, turn your attention to finding a place to put it. Think about the size of the case and its possible location as you are deciding what to put in it. Consider where you'll be sitting when you take time to really enjoy your sit-and-look-at pets. You may wish to build a lower unit. Consider the cost of acrylic for the case and you may wish to build a smaller unit. Consider the lifestyle—vertical or horizontal—of the proposed inhabitant, and you will be able to arrive at a "center of interest dimension" that deserves contemplation. Remember that you'll have to service the terrarium, so don't make the top edge of the case in place on the cabinet come more than armpit high, or you will need a stepladder to get yourself high enough to reach down into the case.

All things considered, simple frame and plank principles can be used to provide the cabinet that will work best for you and your pets. Determine the basic dimensions for the ideal case or tank first. Plan the cabinet top to be at least 2″ larger all around. Try to anticipate what arrangements can be made to accommodate the particular services your pets demand. An extension cord ending in a multiple electrical outlet affixed to the back of the cabinet can allow the electrical needs to stem from one source. (Make sure you have an outlet near enough to plug this cord into.)

You will need storage space for maintenance supplies, as well as food, for your pets. Certain tools will be most easily found if you keep them nearby. A doored section below will keep supplies out of sight yet near to the enclosure where they will be needed. Other tools and equipment might be better kept on open shelves along with some of the books you'll acquire. We show both types of storage, but you can close the base of your cabinet completely or leave it all open. Make one door or two, depending on the cabinet size you figure you need. A door much over 24″ wide takes quite a bit of space to open.

Our basic cabinet design is meant to be adaptable. You can

continue the side supports up or not as you wish. For the anole cabinet/case we show, the two sides support the built-in light box and provide a large shelf area atop it for anything not harmed by a little heat. Anoles need special light bulbs, as do many plants grown indoors and they are also apt to want additional heat, which we supply with 100 watt bulbs. With the front bolts removed, the light box can be swung up, out of the way, for major access to the case.

For an aquarium stand, you may want to make the side supports only as high as the top of the aquarium. For your Insect Zoo in jars, the upright sides can be used to support open shelves.

At any rate, the cabinet shown is basic and can be finished to go with the room you'll put it in. You could even plan it to hold a rodent cage, if you wanted to.

Work out carefully where you are going to locate this piece of furniture, because once it is set up, you aren't going to want to move it around much. Any animal for whom you must create an entire environment needs to have it all prepared and working before he moves in. Check out the equipment and *then* introduce your new pet to his new home. Sit back and watch. Your pet won't write you a thank you note, but you'll know by how quickly he settles down how good a job you've done recreating his homeland for him. You'll know by how long he lives how well you've maintained it.

TERRARIUM CASE WITH LID

Project 12

(see also color plates 10 and 11)

Once you've decided how big a terrarium your sit-and-look-at pet would like, making the bare plastic box is simple. You can even order the $\frac{1}{4}''$ acrylic sheet cut to the exact sizes you need, if you want to.

12-1 Figure your sizes so Front and Back lap the sides, and Front, Back, and Sides sit on top of the Bottom. Sand, but do not polish, the edges to be joined. You'll have to remove the protective paper to tape the parts together for gluing. Take care not to scratch the plastic as you work with it. Run the solvent adhesive into the joints with the applicator for the neatest job. You will have a really fine home for your unpettables if you take the time to polish the edges that are not butted together. To give you some idea of size, the case shown here is 30″ long, 16″ front to back, and 18″ high. A case this large should be reinforced by setting it on a $\frac{3}{4}''$- or 1″-thick plywood base with a keeper frame built tightly around it before you put the weight of gravel, plants, and dirt in.

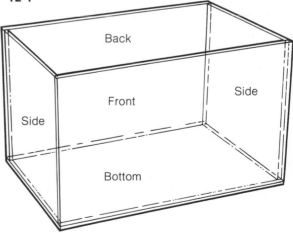

12-2 For a lift-off lid such as we used on the anole case, rabbet ¾″ x 1¼″ S4S stock ¼″ x ⅜″ as shown in the detail. Make a Frame-on-Edge of this so that the rabbet covers the top edge of the plastic case. Cut a piece of Expanded Aluminum—(we used the Veil Decorative Panel in gold)—to lap the frame ⅜″ all around. Hold it in place with a Mitered Flat Frame of Screen Mold, nailed on. If you cannot rabbet stock easily, two pieces of lattice will make up to a similar profile. Make a Frame-on-Edge of ¼″-thick lattice directly on top of the top edge of the plastic case. Fit a Frame-on-Edge of wider lattice around that and glue the pieces together. Mesh can simply be stapled on the top of such a wooden frame, but it looks better if you cover the edges with wood strips.

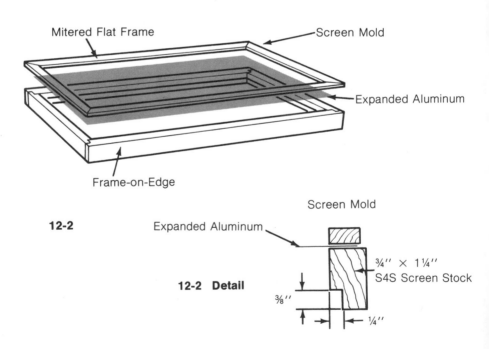

Mitered Flat Frame

Screen Mold

Expanded Aluminum

Frame-on-Edge

12-2

Screen Mold

Expanded Aluminum

12-2 Detail

¾″ × 1¼″ S4S Screen Stock

⅜″

¼″

CABINET FOR CASE Project 13

(see also color plate 10)

Once you've decided what your case is to house, the general approach to building the cabinet for the lizards will apply, whatever specifics you include.

13-1 First, make up the End Planks. Lay out the two Uprights and the necessary Cross Members. Locate the top of the Center Cross Member where you want the top of the lower section to come. Parallel the Uprights with the Long Planks, lapping the inner Cross Member over the Top Cross Member and Uprights. The top of the Finish Block is flush with the top of the Center Cross Member. Set the Top Cleat down from the top of the Finish Block an amount equal to the thickness that the Planked Top will be. Set both Top and Bottom Cleats in from the Back Edge an amount equal to the thickness of the Plywood (or the planking) you will use for the Back. If you plan to have a Divider, as shown, cut three Bottom Cleats now so that they are all the same height and length. If you lay out the two End Planks with front edges together, with the insides facing you, you can locate the Cleats accurately. Add any Cleats needed for shelves. At the same time, cut the Divider and lay it out for cleating. If you use plywood for the Divider, subtract the thickness of the Center Strip from the width of the Divider. The Divider should fit between Center Strip and Plywood Back. Glue and nail the End Planks as soon as you are sure all is square.

13-1

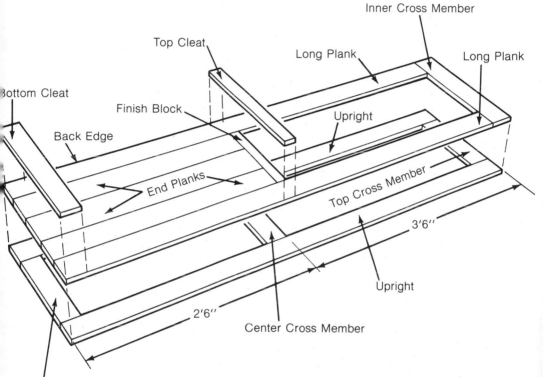

13-2 (Back view) Glue and nail Bottom Planking in place, holding the Uprights temporarily by tacking through a piece of Scrap as shown. The Divider is shown in position, to clarify how it fits.

First, get the Back on. Cut the Plywood Back so it will fit to the floor, to the inside of the End Planks, and to the Underside of the Top Planking. Then cut and fit the Back Frame Members. Then you can glue and nail the Back Frame to the Plywood with proper extensions while all is still flat. That way, it is easy to glue and nail the Back on as a unit. Glue and nail in Bottom Planking, setting in the third Bottom Cleat, if you are using one. Glue and nail on the Top Planking. Set in the Divider and any shelves. Nail through the Top into the Divider Cleat and through the Back into the Divider. It is a good idea to apply glue to the back edge of the Divider before setting it in place.

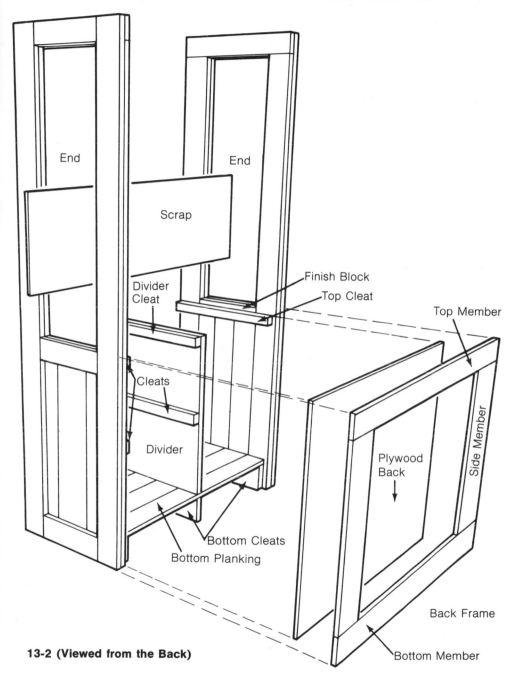

End

End

Scrap

Finish Block

Divider
Cleat

Top Cleat

Top Member

Cleats

Side Member

Divider

Plywood
Back

Bottom Cleats

Bottom Planking

Back Frame

13-2 (Viewed from the Back)

Bottom Member

13-3 Go round to the front. Glue and nail on the Center Strip if you used plywood for the Divider. Nail on Top and Bottom External Battens, making sure you have them parallel.

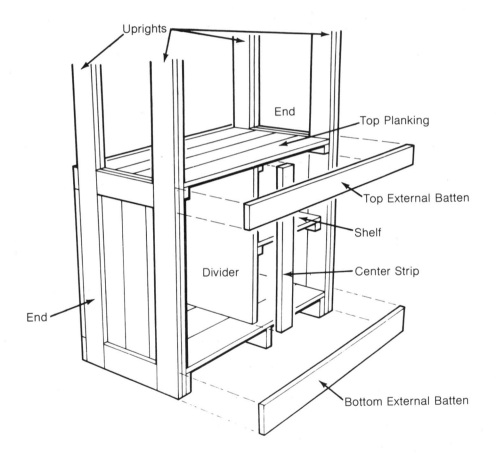

13-3

13-4 Make up Planked Batten Door or Doors as you require, fitting them between the External Battens. You'll need flush overlay cabinet hinges. Follow the manufacturer's directions for easiest installation. If you have only one Door, you won't need a pull.

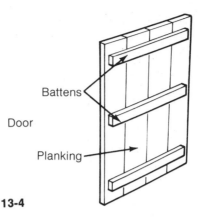

Battens

Door

Planking

13-4

13-5 For sunlovers, a Frame-on-Edge of 1 x 6's with a $\frac{3}{8}''$ plywood Top forms the basic Light Box. Make it to fit in between the ends. We used a stripped-down prewired economy fluorescent fixture for the special light. Cut a piece of flat Aluminum Sheet to the same length as the inside of the Light Box for a Reflector. Force it to bend as you install the fluorescent Fixture. Install porcelain fixtures at the box ends for 100 watt bulbs if you want some heat. Turn the box over before you bolt it on.

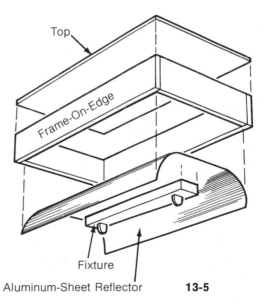

Top

Frame-On-Edge

Fixture

Aluminum-Sheet Reflector

13-5

13-6 Hang the door. Clamp the Light Box high enough above the case top so you'll be able to lift the lid a bit for feeding your pets but not so far above that its light is ineffective. Drill through Uprights and Box Ends, aligning the two Bolt holes in front and the two in back. Check that you won't hit a porcelain fixture. Use $\frac{1}{4}$"-diameter Carriage Bolts with washer and wing nut on each. Remove the two front bolts for the time being, tilt the Light Box up, and reclamp it in the upright position while you set up the terrarium.

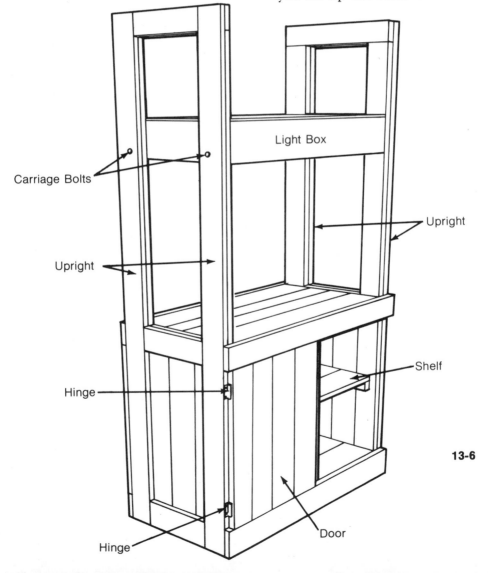

Light Box

Carriage Bolts

Upright

Upright

Shelf

Hinge

Hinge

Door

13-6

CABINET VARIATION FOR TANK Project 14

14-1 The basic cabinet design can easily be adapted to have double doors. With short uprights, it could house an aquarium.

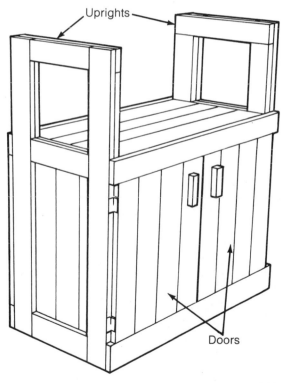

Uprights

Tank Cabinet

Doors

14-1

14-2 Or it can be all shelves, open above for books, an insect zoo in jars, or a tadpole farm.

Shelves

Open Shelves

14-2

RODENT PETS AND THEIR CAGES

Rodent pets do best caged. They cannot be given free run of the house as dogs and cats can because they just don't understand about being housebroken. Children will probably take them out of the cage to pet them and perhaps to let them play, but stay alert. Guinea pigs, hamsters, and gerbils have a couple of other traits in common. They are curious creatures and like nothing better than to explore your home. And they must gnaw to keep their front teeth worn down to usable length. They don't take instruction too well and will gnaw on anything handy—furniture, electric wires, your food. We hope you'll care enough to make sure that what they gnaw on (a) won't hurt them and (b) won't annoy you.

SIZING THE CAGE

Since the rodent resident is usually a child's pet, we suggest you start by measuring the child. The floor is not the best place to set the rodent cage. Putting it on a table or other base is better. We show how to adapt an open-frame table to support a rodent cage. You'll want to consider cage and base together, sized so child and pet can get together easily. Remember, the top of the cage is going to be somewhere between 8″ and 16″ above the top of the base, depending on which rodent we're talking about.

If your child is small, you'll need a much lower table. While you're deciding the cage dimensions you'll want to know how far he can reach. Clamp a board across a doorway and have him stand up to it and reach over and down, if you can't think of any other way to determine the critical figures. You do want the kids to be able to pet their pets kindly, don't you? When the time comes and the new pet is in residence, show the child how to pet it and while you are at it, give lessons in how to pick up the pet without hurting it.

Size the cage so the child can in fact reach a bit beyond the center from one side or another. If it is to stand against a wall, it will have to be narrower and longer so he can reach to the back from the front—or do you plan to do all the cleaning and feeding chores yourself? (If it is going against a wall all the time, there is little point in using transparent acrylic sheet for the back. Use painted hardboard. It's cheaper.) If you want a shelf under the table, one can easily be set on top of the Cross Brace and Bottom Frame Members, or you can omit the Brace and glue and nail on a shelf permanently instead.

GUINEA PIGS

Guinea pigs (cavies) are the largest of the three common rodent pets, a bit on the timid side. They like a little privacy, and if you keep more than one you may find yourself in the real estate business. Sometimes individuals get very possessive and want a little house within the cage all to themselves. Your guinea pig should enjoy the tunnel toy, too. Watch your cavy in action and see if you can figure out what else he might like to play on or with or in. Give him a heavy food dish on the order of the crockery bowls sold for dogs. He's no ballet dancer and tends to be clumsy and knock things over a lot. A ball-point water bottle, the kind meant for small laboratory animals, will suit him fine. These hang on the cage wall; your pet store should have the ones sized for guinea pigs.

None of the rodents should be allowed to sit around on wet litter. That's why the hanging water bottles are suggested. Newspaper or wood shavings are suitable litter/bedding for guinea pigs.

A solitary guinea pig will often come to relate to the person who tends him most. Size your cage/table so that can be the child to whom he belongs. Size your cage to suit both pig and owner. Your average guinea pig needs walls 8" to 12" high and uses 5 or 6 square feet of cage floor area to get enough exercise. Our 30" x 30" floor space works out to just over 6 square feet. Yours might be 24" x 36" for 6 square feet exactly. The pig won't measure, but you will get a fat, lazy pig if you build too small a cage.

CAGE 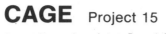 Project 15

(see also color plates 5 and 6)

15-1 The Cage: Beginning
Determine the size Table
Top/Cage Bottom you want
to make. (Actually, the Cage
Bottom takes the place of a
conventional table top.) Cut
$\frac{1}{2}$"-thick Plywood to that
size if the largest dimension
is 3' or less. For a larger one,
use $\frac{3}{4}$"-thick Plywood. Glue
and nail a Flat Frame of
1 x 2's around the under surface of the Cage Bottom so
that the outer edge of the
Frame projects beyond the
Plywood on all four sides an

amount equal to the thickness of the Wall material
that you will use. We used
$\frac{1}{4}$"-thick transparent Acrylic
Sheet for the Walls of the
cage shown. The square of
Plywood measured $29\frac{1}{2}$" less
the width of the saw kerf,
while the outside dimension
of the Flat Frame nailed to
it is 30" x 30".

While the Cage Bottom is
still a flat piece, build a basic
table base to fit it. Then
you'll go back to work on the
Cage.

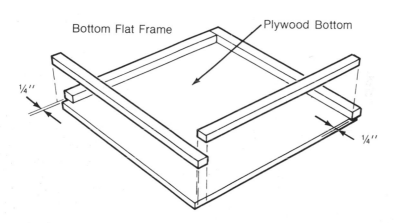

Bottom Flat Frame Plywood Bottom

$\frac{1}{4}$"

$\frac{1}{4}$"

15-1 Table Top/Cage Bottom

BASIC TABLE AND/OR
BASIC BASE Project 16

(see also color plates 5 and 6)

Basic Table

16-1 Building a basic table or base is simple once you have determined the Table Top/Cage Bottom size. Subtract 6″ from the smaller dimension. That, less twice the thickness of the material you'll use for the Apron, is the length of your Outer Frame Top and Bottom pieces. Subtract 6″ from the larger dimension of the Table Top for the length of the Aprons. Subtract twice the thickness of the Outer Frame Bottom Members and that is the length of the Cross Brace. Once you've determined how high you want the table to be, the Inner Frame Sides go from floor to the underside of the Table Top/Cage Bottom while the Outer Frame Sides are that dimension less the width of the Outer Frame Top and the Outer Frame Bottom. For a plywood top, leave the Inner Frame Top loose so it can be used to key the Top to the Base. If you lay out the parts you've cut for the two End Frames as diagrammed, you will know immediately that you're on the right track.

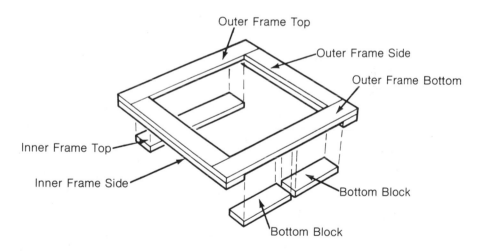

16-1 End Frame

16-2 Glue and nail Aprons to the Front and Back of the End Frames, and set the Cross Brace in place while you do it. Check that the Table Base is square and level. Turn the Table Top/Cage Bottom from 15-1 upside down. Turn the Table Base upside down on top of it. Center the Base. Set the Inner Frame Top pieces in place as indicated here, and glue and nail them to the underside of the Table Top/Cage Bottom. Remove the Table Base and turn it rightside up. Now go on with the cage-making project.

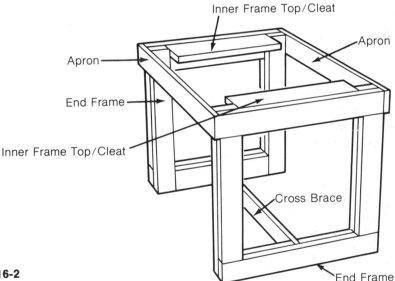

Inner Frame Top/Cleat

Apron

Apron

End Frame

Inner Frame Top/Cleat

Cross Brace

16-2

End Frame

15-2 Back to the Cage

The Acrylic Walls of the cage are held in place by two Flat Frames and four Stretchers. Make the height of the Flat Frame Side Members equal the height of the Acrylic Walls less the thickness of the plywood and the $\frac{1}{4}''$ overlap of wood over Acrylic at the top. (With 12"-high Acrylic, $\frac{1}{2}''$-thick plywood and $\frac{1}{4}''$ overlap, the Side Member here is $11\frac{1}{4}''$ long.) We used $\frac{3}{4}''$ x $1\frac{1}{4}''$ stock for this cage frame, which worked out well since Frame Bottom and Bottom Stretcher came flush with the Bottom Flat Frame of $\frac{3}{4}''$-thick material. You want to have the inside of your Front Flat Frame even with the surface of the Plywood Bottom to make cleaning easiest when the Front Acrylic Wall is removed for housekeeping. So glue and nail the two Flat Frames and the two pairs of Stretchers as shown, keeping the groove around the Plywood Bottom clear, as that is where the Acrylic Walls will fit. Slide the Side Acrylic pieces in position, then the Back Acrylic. Tack a Retainer Strip of Plywood (or hardboard) the same thickness as the Acrylic around sides and back as shown. Then Glue and nail in Inner Back Strip and Side Strips to lap over the Acrylic. Cut the Side Strips $\frac{1}{4}''$ short so the Front Acrylic Wall is retained when it is slipped down into the front Groove. Try to keep Stretchers and Frames, Plywood Retainer Strips and Inner Strips all flush at the top for a better seated Lid.

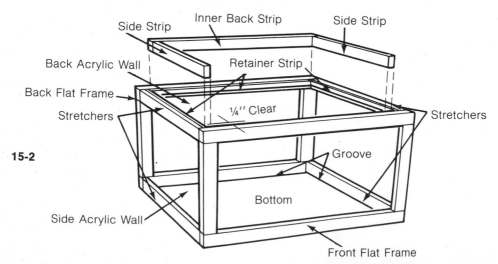

Side Strip

Inner Back Strip

Side Strip

Back Acrylic Wall

Retainer Strip

Back Flat Frame

Stretchers

$\frac{1}{4}''$ Clear

Stretchers

15-2

Groove

Bottom

Side Acrylic Wall

Front Flat Frame

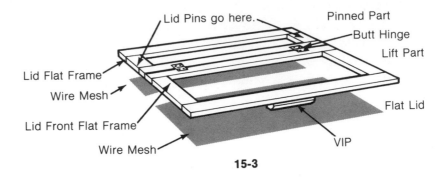

Lid Pins go here.

Pinned Part

Butt Hinge

Lift Part

Lid Flat Frame

Wire Mesh

Lid Front Flat Frame

Wire Mesh

Flat Lid

VIP

15-3

15-3 We made a two-part Lid that is totally removable. You make whatever suits the size and shape of cage best. Make the Flat Lid Frames, gluing and clamping them flat. Turn them face down and staple ½″ Wire Mesh (galvanized hardware cloth) to the underside of both Frames. We put the selvage edge under the Hinge joint. The other edges are kept from the animal completely as they fall over the wooden parts of the walls.

Even so, you'll want to watch out for any wire that might be bent out. Bend it into the wood as best you can. Align the two meshed Frames and install 1½″ or 2″ x 1″ or so Butt Hinges on the top surface. The VIP is simply a Very Important Piece that is rounded enough to permit the Hinges to work. It catches the center of the Front Plastic and holds it secure against the Front Frame.

15-4 Set the Cage on the Table or Base. Slide in the Front Acrylic Wall. Set the Lid on the Cage. Drill through the smaller section of the Lid into the Stretcher on either side, for a tight fit on a $\frac{1}{8}''$ or $\frac{3}{16}''$-diameter Dowel. Round off the end of the Dowel and set it through the hole, gluing it into the Lid. Cut off flush to the Lid surface. Do the same on the other side of the Cage. Now the Lid stays in place when you lift the front section but you can still lift off the entire two-section Lid should you want to. You can provide a Latch for the cage in the same way or use a short piece of wire. Just drill through the Front Lid Frame (above the Acrylic) into the VIP. Insert the Latch Pin.

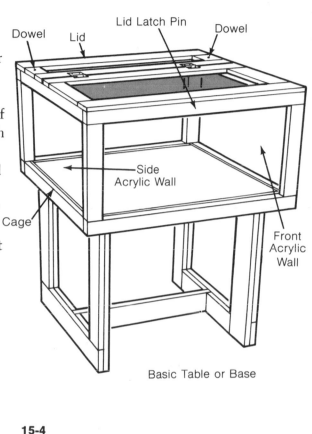

Dowel Lid Lid Latch Pin Dowel

Side Acrylic Wall

Cage

Front Acrylic Wall

Basic Table or Base

15-4

Children will enjoy helping you get the cage ready for the new inmate. You will need cage litter and/or bedding of cedar or other shavings, a food bowl, water, and a little house of some sort. You can build a bungalow like the one shown on the next page, or you can use a low-rent cardboard box. Whatever you do, reassure the young child when the new guinea pig hides in the house and falls asleep. He doesn't mean to be unfriendly—he's just bashful. Be patient.

BUNGALOW Project 17

(see also color plates 5 and 6)

You'll need ⅛"-thick acrylic sheet to duplicate the guinea pig bungalow we show. Two colors are most attractive. For the roof, one piece 9" wide x 14" long will make both front and back sections. We used yellow. You can make the walls from one piece 9" wide x 26" long.

17-1 The key for the bungalow lies in cutting two Ends to the pattern shown. You will also need a Back 7¾" long by 3¼" high and a Front 7¾" long and 5½" high, with a doorway in the center. Doorways for most guinea pigs should be between 3" x 3" and 4" x 4". The guinea pig will enlarge it with his teeth anyway. The roof takes a Front Roof Piece 9" x 6" and a Back Roof Piece 9" x 8".

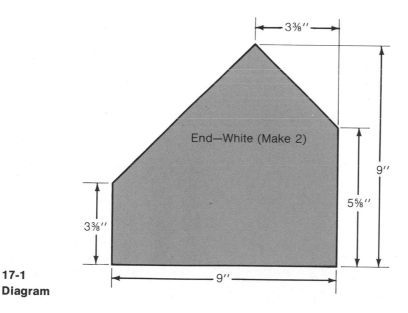

End—White (Make 2)

17-1 Diagram

17-2 Be careful to have the Front and Back lap over the Ends, as shown in the diagram. Tape and glue up the four walls first. Tape the Back Roof Piece in place as shown and then glue it on. The Front Roof Piece also is set down $3/8''$ from the peak and should be taped and glued in place, as shown by the broken lines. Hold the pieces together. Use your square or at least use a squared wood block to keep joints true as you run the solvent adhesive in. Once the adhesive sets, you can clean off any residue of tape adhesive with lighter fluid. Waxing the plastic makes it easier to keep clean. Make another bungalow in different colors for a second pig.

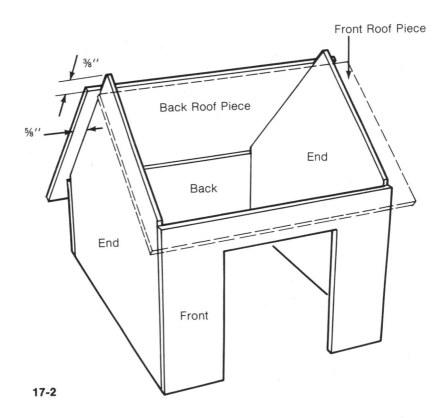

Front Roof Piece

$3/8''$

Back Roof Piece

$5/8''$

End

Back

End

Front

17-2

TUNNEL TOY Project 18

(see also color plate 5)

18-1 A toy for a guinea pig doesn't need to be very complicated. Your pet will be quite happy going in and out of a tunnel, and once in a while he might make it up to the Roof. To duplicate the tunnel toy we show, you'll need a piece of ⅛"-thick acrylic sheet, 8" x 24". Cut the Roof first. (Cut a piece to 12" x 8", then make the two cuts in to the internal corner as indicated by the cut arrows on the Pattern.) Save the cut-out piece. All the Walls are 4" high.

Wall A is 11⅞" long, Wall B is 8" long (use the cut out) Wall C is 7⅞", and Wall D is 4⅛". Join Walls A and B and join Walls C and D. Then the paired Walls can be taped and glued to the Roof. We showed the toy upside down so you would be able to see which wall abuts which wall to make the dimensions work out right. You may want to make two or three such tunnels and let your pig run through them like a maze. Turn one upside down and see what happens.

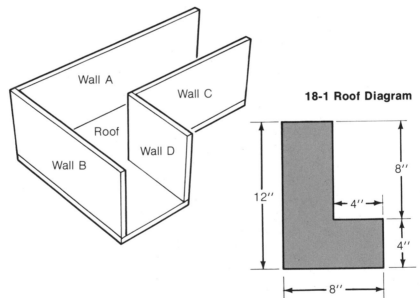

18-1 Roof Diagram

18-1

HAMSTERS

Hamsters are perhaps the most community minded of the three rodent types included here. A cage 24″ x 18″ is probably the minimum size for one hamster; you can figure about one square foot each for more than one. Walls should be at least 12″ high; 14″ is better. The cage we show is large enough for your hamster and three or four of his siblings. They'll have a ball running up the wire mesh ends and down the slide, and rocking on the rocker stair—before they demolish all the toys with their teeth. It's not a destructive urge, just pure necessity. Gnawing is their nature. Give them plenty to gnaw on so they can keep their molars to manageable length. The plastic house is not immune to destruction. You're apt to find your hamsters all huddled in the house asleep in the daytime and busy enlarging the doorway at night.

Hamsters do best on commercial and dry foods. Remember, they are hoarders, and moist hoarded food often rots. You will throw away any spoiled hoard when you clean the cage once a week, but don't toss out everything your pet has stashed away. He needs his nose to tell him it's his cage. You'll keep him guessing, alert, and active enough if you make new toys for him to exercise on.

It's a good idea to rotate hamster toys. Take out an old one and put in a new one to keep them on their toes. A commercial hamster wheel can be mounted on the acrylic back of the cage, and you can build a slide/tunnel toy or rocker stair for starters. Hamsters will treat their little house as a toy, too.

You can also keep them guessing as to how the cage is latched if you use double-headed staging nails to pin the lid, front and back, as shown in the drawings. Remove the front pins and the lid will "hinge up" on the back pins—if you've rounded off the bottom edge of the lid properly. We show a totally separate lift-off lid in the photograph, dowel-pinned on so the hamsters would have to organize themselves into work crews to lift it.

Keep a rock on it if you worry. The end panels of the cage are removable, but secure the hamsters before you try to clean their cage completely. (A hamster will have a hard time climbing out of a large can or jar. They're not too good at leaping, although compared to guinea pigs, they're Olympic acrobats.) We used ¼"-thick acrylic sheet for front, back, and bottom, because it is easily cleaned. You may want something less expensive for the bottom piece, but make sure it is cut to hold the bottom edge of the transparent front and back in place.

CAGE Project 19

19-1 Building the cage requires making up a series of Frames that fit together. Start by making one as shown, the size of the Bottom Sheet you've selected plus the thicknesses of Front and Back Acrylic Walls. Glue and nail it together. Acrylic Sheet and most other panel materials will require the inside Joists about every 12″, as shown. Surround them with a Frame-on-Edge. We used ³⁄₄″ x 1¼″ stock.

While this cage is designed as a unit to be set on a table or cabinet, you could make it as a Table Top/Cage Bottom unit similar to the guinea pig Cage/Table unit. Just anchor your Cage Bottom Frame to a suitably sized Basic Table Base. Two additional Joists with the Inner Frame Top of the Table projecting down would do the trick easily.

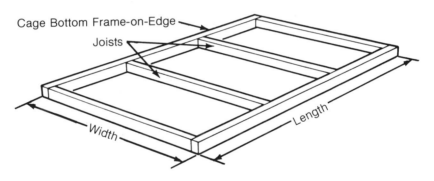

19-1

19-2 Make up a Front Flat Frame and a Back Flat Frame the same length as your Bottom Frame and the height of your acrylic material plus the thickness of the Bottom Frame. Hamsters need action space between 12″ and 15″ in height. The bottom members of the Front and Back Frames must be higher than the thickness of your Bottom Frame plus the thickness of the Bottom Acrylic Sheet. We made these of $\frac{3}{4}$″ x $1\frac{1}{2}$″ stock; the Top and Side Frame members are made of $\frac{3}{4}$″ x $1\frac{1}{4}$″ material. Glue and nail Front and Back Frames to the Bottom Frame. Check that Front and Back Acrylic Walls fit flat and tight against them when Bottom Sheet is positioned. Notch the two Spreaders to hold the top of the Acrylic Walls and position the Frames top edges. Glue and nail them on securely. Put the nails well in from the ends of the Spreaders (not into the Acrylic though) so there'll be clear room to drill for the staging nail Pins if you use them. You can see from the drawing how easy cleaning the cage will be. Just sweep everything out when one of the End Panels is removed (see 19-3). If you have facilities for bending acrylic, the Front, Bottom, and Back can be made in one piece, giving you a rounded corner rather than a square one to clean.

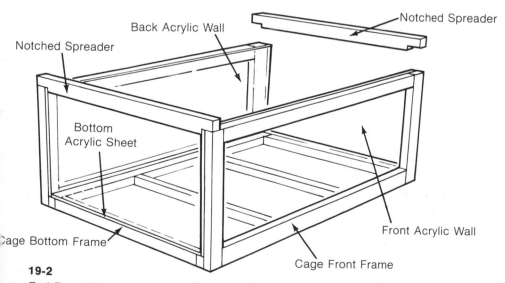

19-2
End Panel Removed, as For Cleaning

19-3 Glue and clamp together End Panel Frames of light material like screen stock, to which ½″ galvanized wire mesh can be stapled. Let the edges of the mesh lap the wood Frame so the raw edge falls between End Frame and Cage proper.

The best solution for the removable End Panel might be to use threaded inserts in the Front and Back Frames. Use epoxy glue to fasten a wing nut to a machine bolt, for a threaded bolt you can remove without tools.

Your gnawing hamsters will have the wire to contend with on the Ends, the plastic on Front, Back, and Bottom. Keep your eye on the Notched Spreaders, though, lest they go to work on those. Make up a Flat Frame for the Lid now too, rounding off the lower corners as shown for hinging action. Staple Wire Mesh to the underside of the Lid, so that the raw edges are tucked away when the Lid is closed. If you make your cage length such that a full wide piece of mesh can be used, you won't have any raw metal edges available to be any danger to the caged hamster.

Use wood shavings for litter; newspaper will do if you keep it very dry. If the fallout through the mesh annoys you, a strip of acrylic can be added outside the wire mesh on both End Panels. You'll need some strips or blocks of screen molding to hold it in place, but don't close in the whole End Panel. Your hamsters need the air and the climbing opportunities the mesh permits.

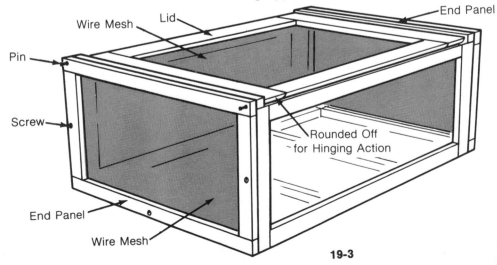

19-3

HOUSE Project 20

Your hamster can probably fit into a paper box 4" x 4" x 3" high if he curls up tight, but if you want to build him a more comfortable house, make it a bit bigger than that. To duplicate the one we show, you'll need one piece of ⅛"-thick acrylic sheet 9" x 10½" of whatever color you want for the roof and another piece 6" x 18" for the walls. We used white for the roof, yellow for the walls.

20-1 Cut two 6" x 6" pieces for Front and Back. Cut the 3" x 3" triangles off them both, as shown. On the piece for the Front only, cut out the doorway 3" wide and rounded on top as shown. You'll need two identical Sides. Make them each 5¾" long by 3" high.

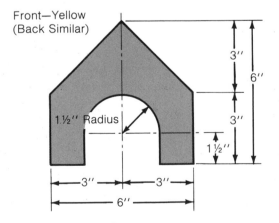

20-1

20-2 Use your square or a wood block to get the corners true as you fabricate a square of the wall parts, letting the Sides fit between the Front and Back. Then tape and glue the two Roof Pieces, each 9″ x 5¼″, in place.

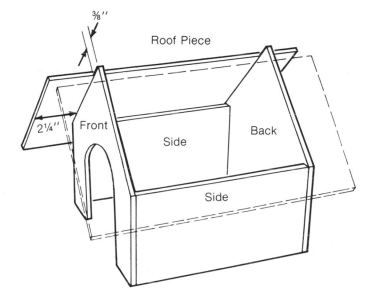

20-2

OUTHOUSE Project 21

21-1 For the outhouse, you'll need a wide-mouthed jar big enough for your hamster to turn around in, and some scraps of ⅛″-thick acrylic. The two Sides are of white plastic in the one shown; 3″ x 4″ pieces suited the length of the jar we used. The easiest way to make the Front and Back is to use a circle cutter with a blade for plastics or a compass with a scriber point and a coping saw. Either way, cut the circle out of the center of a piece of plastic 5″ x 6″, then cut the plastic in half, giving you two pieces 3″ x 5″ with half a circle missing from each. Fit your jar between the Front and Back to see how much slant you can give the Sides. Tape and glue all four plastic pieces together. Put the facility in the corner your hamster has already selected for his toilet. He'll get the idea, and you will have a glass jar to wash out once a day instead of messy litter to pick up.

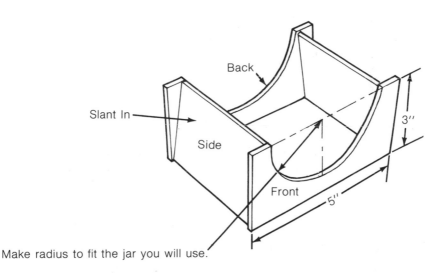

Back

Slant In

Side

3″

Front

5″

Make radius to fit the jar you will use.

21-1

22-1 The circle you cut out for the outhouse might make a rolly toy for gerbils, but it is not likely to be big enough for a rocker stair for hamsters. For them, you need a circle about 8″ in diameter to cut in half for the Sides. Make two toys if you want different colored Sides. You'll need scrap pieces of ⅛″-thick plastic about 4″ long for Platform and Steps. Make them all exactly the same length; anywhere from 3″ to 4½″ is good. You'll want one piece 3″ wide for the Platform, four pieces 1¼″ wide for the Steps. You'll probably find it easier to glue up this project if you use wood blocks to hold the Platform and Steps properly spaced and aligned. Curved side down, it rocks. Flat side down, it is a step-right-up toy that your hamsters will run up and down when they are not busy with their slide/tunnel.

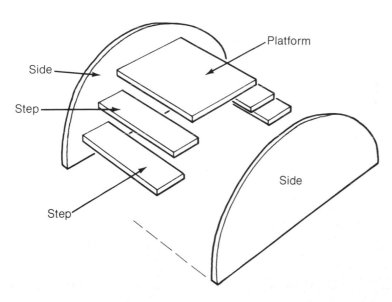

Platform

Side

Side

Step

Step

22-1

23-1 The key to the slide/ tunnel toy is the large plastic triangles. You'll need two, just alike. Cut an 11¼″ square in half diagonally. Cut a doorway in each triangle as shown. Turn one of them over so the doorway is at the left. (We call that the Back in our assembly diagram.) You'll need some strips 3″ wide, too; one 10⅛″ long for the Stair Back, one 10″ long for the Slide, and four pieces, each 6″ long, for the two Tents.

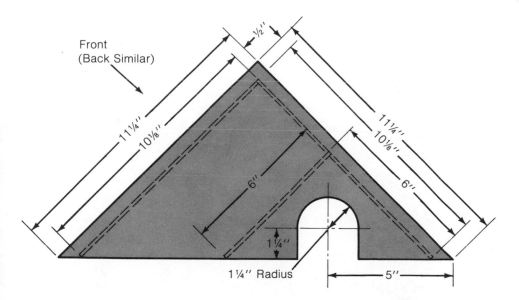

23-1 Diagram

23-2 Tape and glue the two larger strips together at right angles to each other, letting the 10″ Slide butt against the Stair Back. Tape that assembly between the two large Back and Front triangles so bottom edges are all flush. Glue. Make up the two Tents. Affix Tent A centered over the Front Door and Tent B over the Back Door. You'll find your hamsters can climb 3″ lengths of Solid Acrylic Rod, $\frac{1}{4}$″ in diameter, glued to the Stair Back at $1\frac{3}{8}$″ intervals, center to center. Your hamsters will discover the hiding holes at the end of the tunnel—under the Slide and under the Stair Back—and hide. See how long it takes before they go up the Stair and down the Slide. Remember, they aren't graduates of Hamster Day School, so you'll either have to show them or wait until they discover what fun it is by themselves.

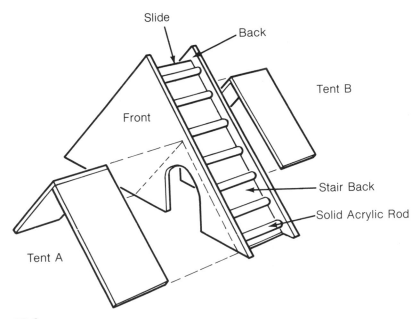

23-2

GERBILS

A whole gerbil family needs a minimum of two square feet of floor space and a height of 8″ to 12″ for their cage. We were doubly generous and built this cage to use up a 2′ x 4′ sheet of ¼″-thick acrylic. You can often juggle sizes within the range acceptable to the particular pet you wish to house in order to utilize materials you have on hand. Most pets, especially the rodents, aren't finicky about the shape of their cage—long and narrow or exactly square—as long as it gives them enough room to run around. You can be the finicky one and build it to fit the space you wish to fill.

Do measure the zookeeper first, though, before you make a final decision. Cages set directly on the floor are often subject to too much draft for small rodents. A low table is apt to be better for all concerned. You may already have an old coffee table that will be just the right place for a gerbil cage.

Remember one advantage of making the cage larger than minimum: if there is room inside the cage, the temptation to take the gerbils out to play is lessened. Escaped gerbils (and hamsters for that matter) are the subject of U.S.D.A. warnings. Stray families of such rodents can multiply enough to be a real danger to crops. Teach the young child to be gentle with his gerbil, to scoop him up with two hands, not lift him by his tail. Gerbils do like people and, being diurnal, are apt to be active when the kids are up and about.

CAGE  Project 24

24-1 You'll see from the names of the parts that this gerbil cage is made the same way as the hamster cage. We cut out acrylic sheet to 24" x 24" for the Bottom and 12" x 24" for Front and Back. Build your Bottom Frame first. Glue and nail on Front and Back Frames. Check Acrylic Front and Back Walls with the Bottom Sheet in place. Notch the two Spreaders to secure the Front and Back Frames in position. Make up the End Frames with ¼" galvanized Wire Mesh the same way as described for hamsters with ½" Mesh. Again, the Lid can be either a totally removable pegged-in-place Lid, as shown in the photographs, or be Pinned front and back to lift like a hinged Lid or come off completely. If you plan to let your kids take the Lid off, make the sides at least 10" high—gerbils can jump. They are also very curious and will enjoy the many hiding places and queer-shaped spaces built into the gerbil gym.

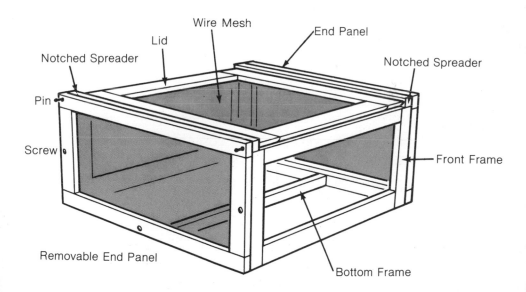

24-1

GYM Project 25

(see also color plate 4)

What they lack in size, gerbils make up for in speed. Quick, darting moves and now-you-see-me, now-you-don't type peek-a-boo games will delight both you and your gerbil. He'll run up, slide down, and hide, jump into the Bin filled high with shavings, exercise on the Wheel you can mount on the End Wall, simply sleep in the Tunnel or under the Ramps, and munch all the time on whatever is handy, sitting back on his haunches and holding food in his tiny fingers. As is true for all the rodents, having short lengths of hardwood dowels loose in the cage is a good idea. He can satisfy his gnawing needs on such expendable toys. It won't entirely keep him from chewing on the gym you've built, but perhaps it will help to satisfy his very real need to gnaw in a way less upsetting to the gym builder.

25-1 You'll need ⅛″-thick acrylic sheet to duplicate the gym shown. We used red, white, and black with a yellow Exercise Wheel. The End Wall is 8¼″ by 9″. The three Bin Sides require a strip 17¾″ long, tapering from 5″ to 3″. Each of the two Pillars is 8¼″ long by 1½″ wide, the Tunnel Back is 3″ x 6″, and the Bottom Run and Ramps can be cut from a strip 12″ long by 3″ wide. All these parts are in white. Red pieces include the Tunnel Run at 3″ x 12″; End, 3″ x 3″; Slide, 2⅞″ x 7¾″; and Stair, 3″ x 7¾″; plus two Step Strips of 3″ x ⅜″ each. The Bin Back is 6″ x 8¼″ while the Tunnel Top is 3″ x 12″, both these parts in black. The key to this project is the Bin. Cut the three side pieces first to specifications shown.

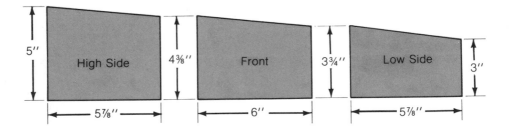

25-1

25-2 Tape the Bin Sides and Back in a square—and make sure you have it really square. It should measure 6″ x 6″ outside when glued up. All the other parts fit around it.

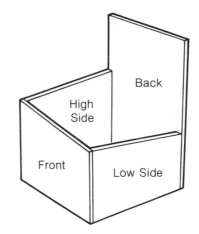

25-2 Bin Parts Diagram

25-3 Assemble Tunnel Top, Tunnel Run, Tunnel Back, and End, using a wood block to steady the opposite end while you glue this much together. Add the Pillars to this assembly, overlapping them halfway onto the Tunnel Back. Sand the ends of the Ramps so they will fit against the ends of the Bottom Run when it is set up 2″ as shown. Tape and glue. Position the Ramp-Run-Ramp sub-assembly between the Pillars and the previously assembled Bin. Tape and glue.

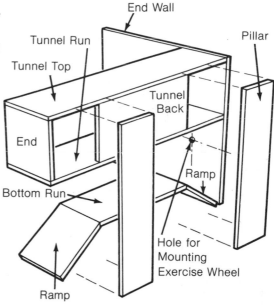

25-3

25-4 It is easier to drill the End Wall for the Exercise Wheel before you glue the Wall in place. Check out the Wheel before you buy it. Can it be attached to the ⅛″-thick acrylic? Most are meant to clamp onto a wire cage or sit on their own stand. The one we used worked fine on the acrylic. Check the dimensions for locating the mounting hole after you've got the wheel, making sure there will be room to tighten the wing nut under the Tunnel Run. If you think the first wheel you find won't work for you, shop around. The plastic ones are a bit quieter than the all-metal ones, too. Sand the ends of the Slide and Stair so they will fit properly against the edges of the Tunnel Run. Tape the End Wall in place with the Slide set in between End Wall and Bin. Glue. Add the Step Strips to the Stair and tape and glue that assembly in place against the Bin as shown. When the glue has set, attach the Wheel and set the whole thing in the cage. Watch while your gerbil investigates and tries out his new gym.

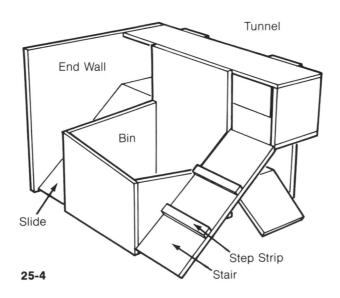

Tunnel

End Wall

Bin

Slide

Step Strip

Stair

25-4

THREE

Enjoying the Results

ENJOYING YOUR PET STARTS WHEN YOU SELECT one whose needs and desires you feel you'll be able to meet willingly, whose life-style echoes yours, and whose affection-response complements your own.

The choice of pets is wide—from the exotic foreign reptile to the homeless stray, there's a variety available to suit every family who really wants a pet.

Some people think dogs are the only pets to have. If you are aquainted with one who responds to you, understands your moods, and knows when you need to talk aloud, your pet has selected you. There are cat people who admire the sense of self-reliance cats often have, who like the tolerant attitude many cats display toward their owners. Still others champion a bird or two, on the grounds that they are small, inexpensive to keep, sensitive, playful, and make good company without requiring daily trips outdoors.

Though they may not express their appreciation of your efforts as directly as some other animals, rodents may be chosen for a number of reasons. Without the company of another of their own kind, they are capable of displaying affection toward the human most involved with supplying their daily needs. A rodent family will entertain and amuse you and is a good vehicle for a living lesson in the mammalian life cycle. Their care is routine enough for the youngest human keeper—with an adult standing by, please.

More demanding because you must be responsible for their total environment, sit-and-look-at pets have a different appeal. The most familiar pet in this group is, of course, the aquarium fish. Whether they are fancy salt-water tropicals or more local fresh-water fish, they obviously are not pettable pets, but their actions can be aesthetically pleasing and their care exacting. Though not much on expressing affection, fish often seem to their owners to have distinct personalities. Adding animal life to a terrarium is the way to include another whole group of un-pettable pets. Herpetology can easily become a most intriguing leisure-time interest. Frogs, lizards, snakes, and turtles may not be terribly affectionate, but they do mean that people whose allergies prevent them from tolerating a furry friend need not go petless. These animals lead quaint, surprising lives and let you into their secret world once you've provided the right setting.

RESPONSIBLE OWNERS AND RESPONSIVE PETS

It's not enough just to build the cage, even if you do fill it with wonderful toys for your pet. Providing bed and board is an ongoing process. You need to be concerned with all aspects of your pet's life, so that he will enjoy living in the housing you've provided for him.

Maintaining the environment your pet needs means not only getting filtered water running for your anole but moving the dog deck spring and fall to take advantage of cooler summer breezes and warmer, sheltered positions in winter. It means making sure the perches are dry before you put them back in the flight cage, providing clean bedding when needed for your rodents, restraining your cat so he doesn't become a highway fatality.

There are further responsibilities of pet ownership to be considered, too. First, is the pet you contemplate owning legal where you live? For example, you can't buy turtles in New Jersey, and gerbils are outlawed in California. No poisonous or dangerous pet should be kept in anyone's home. There are license and leash laws almost everywhere concerning dogs, and, more and more, cats are coming under the same ordinances. Local board of health rulings often limit the number of these pets per household.

Limiting pet populations is fast becoming a major concern of organizations engaged in promoting kindness to all animals. The growing number of unwanted stray dogs and cats is too much of a burden on many municipalities; the practice of dumping the unwanted offspring of a summer mating in the vacation community is especially inconsiderate. Far better to have your animal spayed or neutered if you will not be able to provide the offspring with a proper home. In many communities, organizations are taking steps to reduce the cost of these services. You'll want to watch it with the selection of your rodent pets, too. After all, one of the reasons they are used as laboratory animals is their ability to reproduce quickly. If you don't want to be inundated by a sea of hamsters, don't house a male and a female together.

We might plead here, too, for our friends in the forest and on the shore. Please leave them there. People who live at the edge of the woods almost inadvertently become foster folks for young or injured local wildlife—and just as often run afoul of local fish and wildlife laws. Wild animals have no place in the pet world. You can't really provide the environment needed without the staff and space of an up-to-date zoo. Even trying to provide for orphaned young animals is a chore best left to a veterinarian or conservation officer with experience. The more closely the animal's habitat can be imitated, the more quickly he can be set free. The baby deer you "found" in the tall grass was probably left there while his mother ranged further for food. You are very likely causing her anguish by mistakenly trying to be kind to her offspring. An injured racoon will fare far better in local hands than it will back in your town apartment.

Everyone will be happier if you stick to pets that will appreciate your ministrations, especially if those ministrations are under the guidance of your local veterinarian. He can tell you what inoculations are advisable, if your town's ordinances don't give you that information. If you learn more about the pets you get, you will recognize certain signals of distress in time. You will get a sense of what is normal behavior for that animal, and any marked deviation should be cause for reasonable concern.

Once you know what your pet likes, you can decide what to build very easily. Enjoy the building activity. Let your pet enjoy the results. You'll be proud to transport your cat in an aluminum and wood case you built; to watch your dog relax above the mud on the redwood deck you built for him; to see your birds fly in front of their own mural. Your guinea pig will have a bungalow unlike any other, your lizards will have the best waterfall you could build, and you will enjoy their enjoyment.

FOUR

Sources: Information and Materials

In addition to advice from your veterinarian, you'll probably want at least one care and feeding book about the animal of your choice. If you are totally unfamiliar with the pet you have in mind, do read a book—preferably several books—before you get the pet. You'll have no problem finding dog- and cat-care books at libraries and bookstores. Some material is also available from pet food suppliers. It is a good idea to give the young owner of a new puppy or kitten a feeding/caring for/training-book written specifically for that child's age level. That will provide some source of authority for the responsibilities of owning a pet. A number of recent pet books are aimed at children and there are some beautifully written and illustrated titles in this area.

BOOKS ABOUT ANIMALS

Some of the books we borrowed from the Sussex County (N.J.) Library—whose staff was remarkably efficient in digging out references—were very well done, and the best of these were in the children's section. Look for:

CARAS, ROGER. *A Zoo in Your Room.* New York: Harcourt Brace Jovanovich, 1975.

Delightfully illustrated by Pamela Johnson, beautifully written, this book is a good answer for the child who is teasing for an unusual type of pet.

HOKE, JOHN. *Terrariums.* New York: Franklin Watts, 1972.

———. *Aquariums.* New York: Franklin Watts, 1975.

These are both quite matter-of-fact and complete, probably written with school science classes in mind. They are well illustrated and useful for home installations. These are among the few pet books that give enough how-to information so that you can actually do what they suggest.

ROOD, RONALD. *May I Keep This Clam, Mother? It Followed Me Home.* New York: Simon and Schuster, 1973.

———. *How Do You Spank a Porcupine?* New York: Simon and Schuster, 1969.

Mr. Rood lives at the edge of a forest, and he has good answers for the camping trips that result in "can't we keep the baby skunk?" questions.

SILVERSTEIN, ALVIN AND VIRGINIA. *Guinea Pigs, All About Them.* New York: Lothrop, Lee, and Shepard, 1972.

———. *Hamsters, All About Them.* New York: Lothrop, Lee, and Shepard, 1974.

Very informative. The photographs by Frederick Breda show happy, intelligent animals enjoying life and make you want to own rodents, too.

Among adult books, titles seem to run more to reminiscences about favorite pets than to helpful care-and-feeding books. The following two exceptions may be useful to you.

FOX, MICHAEL W. *Understanding Your Dog.* New York: Coward McCann, 1972.

―――. *Understanding Your Cat.* New York: Coward McCann, 1974.

   Dr. Fox says a good deal to help you understand what ails your dog or cat.

We have found two series of reasonably inexpensive books, readily available through pet stores, that will give you basic information to start with. A self-addressed stamped envelope to the following will bring you an order blank listing the titles available in the two series:

> The Pet Library, Ltd.
> 600 South Fourth St.
> Harrison, N.J. 07029

> TFH Publications, Inc.
> 211 West Sylvania Ave.
> Neptune, N.J. 07753

For a listing of inexpensive booklets on vivariums and their most likely inhabitants, enclose a stamped self-addressed envelope when you write to:

> Small Worlds-Vivariums, Inc.
> 107 East 88th St.
> New York, N. Y. 10028

INFORMATION FROM THE PET INDUSTRY

If you send 25¢ to whichever of the following two addresses is closest to you, you will receive a brief but authoritative little *Pet Care Book.* It contains information about the basic needs of cage birds, fish, hamsters, gerbils, and guinea pigs.

Geisler   Geisler
3902 Leavenworth St.   30 Valentino Rd.
Omaha, Neb. 68105   Fairfield, N.J. 07006

A stamped self-addressed envelope enclosed with your letter of inquiry to the following will bring you a note on the current availability of information from these two pet-food manufacturers:

Gaines Dog Research Center
White Plains, N.Y. 10602

Ralston Purina Company
Consumer Products Group
Checkerboard Square
St. Louis, Mo. 63188

Ralston Purina has two small but very good books, one a handbook on dog care and the other on cats.

INFORMATION ABOUT BUILDING

BASIC BUILDING BOOKS

You wouldn't be building these projects for your pets if you didn't like to build things. We have tried to keep it simple so that any of these projects can be completed with only common hand tools as equipment, but it is certainly true, as with most project building, that power tools make shorter work of cutting, shaping, and smoothing operations. The whole "crate craft" system is based on straight sawcuts, easily achieved with a hand saw but more quickly performed with a power saw. If working with wood is new to you, you will need more fundamental information than is contained in this book.

CAMPBELL, ROBERT, AND N.J. MAGER, eds. *How To Work With Tools and Wood.* Pocket Books, 1947. (Distributed by the Stanley Company.)

LABARGE, LURA. *Crate Craft.* New York: Butterick, 1976. The general information sections will be useful to you.

BOOKLETS FROM MANUFACTURERS

Repair, Improve, Create with Reynolds Do-It-Yourself Aluminum. It is available from your local hardware store/home center at a suggested retail price of $1.95, or write to:

Reynolds Metals Company
Building Products Division
Consumer Hardware Products
Richmond, Va. 23261

Do It Yourself with Plexiglas Acrylic Sheet. Send 50¢ in check or money order to:

Rohm and Haas
P.O. Box 9730
Philadelphia, Pa. 19104

If your power tools are new to you, write to the manufacturer for a list of the books he would recommend, and study the operator's manual for each tool. You may wish to write to other manufacturers for information they make available to consumers. A stamped self-addressed envelope enclosed with your inquiry usually brings a faster response.

SOURCES OF SUPPLIES

We list below the product and the manufacturer where a specific item was used in these projects, though without necessarily implying that the listed item is the only one that will work.

Homasote®
    (doghouse surfacing)

Homasote
Box 7240
West Trenton, N.J. 08628

Exterior Latex in New England Red
    (doghouse paint)

Cook and Dunn Paint Corp.
161 Kossuth
Newark, N.J. 07101

Midget Louvers®
    (doghouse vents)

Midget Louver Company
800 Main Ave.
Norwalk, Conn. 06852

Do-It-Yourself® Aluminum
   Lincane pattern
      (natural on cat window-seat, gold anodized on bed/carrier)
   Decorator Panel expanded aluminum
      (Veil pattern, vivarium lid)
      (Vista pattern, flight cage)
   Plain aluminum sheet in natural finish (light box)

Reynolds Metals Company
Consumer Hardware Products
P.O. Box 27003
Richmond, Va. 23261

¼″ Plexiglas® clear
    (dog deck windscreen, terrarium, all three rodent cages)

Consult your yellow pages for local distributors.

⅛″ Plexiglas® in colors
(bird feeder, rodent toys
and accessories)

Consult your yellow pages
for local distributors.

Masonite®
(brand of hardboard
used on cat bed/carrier,
bird flight cage back,
etc.)

Masonite Corp.
29 North Wacker Dr.
Chicago, Ill. 60606

No. 50 Steel Timber-
Topper®
(lumber cattrees)
No. 52 Hardwood Timber-
Topper®
(natural cattrees)

The Brewster Corporation
Old Saybrook, Conn. 06475

#4 Venetian Blind Cord,
Glazed
(Fawn and Apple Green
are colors used on
cattrees shown.)

Wellington Puritan Mills, Inc.
Madison, Ga. 30650

Woven wire mesh, galvanized
(¼″ wire mesh for
gerbils, ⅜″ or ½″ for
hamsters and guinea
pigs)

Stock item made by a num-
ber of companies. Also called
hardware cloth. This is *not*
insect screening. Hardware
and garden supply sources
usually carry it with their
chickenwire and fencing
materials.

Brass Finish, Gothic
Swag-Lite Chain with Lam-
parts Loop connectors
(bird cage suspension)

Angelo Brothers Co.
159 West Allegheny Ave.
Philadelphia, Pa. 19154

Adhesives
   wood to wood

Franklin Glue Co.
2020 Bruck
Columbus, O. 43207

   acrylics

Buy your adhesive where you
buy your acrylic sheet.

   safe in water
Duro® Silicone Sealer
   (for waterfall)

Woodhill Chemical
18731 Cranwood Pkwy.
Cleveland, O. 44128

Dynaflo™ Model 410 Motor
Filter
   (for waterfall)

Metaframe Corp.
41 Slater Drive
East Paterson, N.J. 07407

Vitalite® bulb
   (for vivarium)

Duro-Test Corp.
2321 Kennedy Blvd.
North Bergen, N.J. 07047

Cedar cage carpets
   (for birds)

Geisler Pet Products
(see bibliography)

Oasis®
   ball-point water bottles
   (for hamster and guinea
   pig)

Oasis Pet Products
461 Walnut St.
Napa, Calif. 94558

Mr. Shag rugs
   (for cattrees)

Solomon White Co.
Dalton, Ga. 30720

If you can't find a local source for acrylic sheet, it is sold by mail order by the following firms. Please write (with enclosed stamped self-addressed envelope) for price quotations, information, etc.

Ain Plastics, Inc.
160 S. MacQuesten Parkway
Mount Vernon, N.Y. 10550

Mail Order Plastics
56 Lispenard St.
New York, N.Y. 10013

If you can't find the Timber-Toppers® locally, write to the manufacturer—he will fill mail orders.

If you can't find something locally, try the following for tools, cabinetware, and many specialty items available by mail order. Write them directly, requesting the price of their current mail order catalogs.

Albert Constantine
2056 Eastchester Rd.
Bronx, N.Y. 10461

Craftsman Wood Service
2729 South Mary St.
Chicago, Ill. 60608

Minnesota Woodworkers Supply Co.
Industrial Blvd.
Rogers, Minn. 55374

Both Sears Roebuck's and Montgomery Ward's catalogs include many of these items.

METRIC EQUIVALENCY CHART
Converting Inches to Centimeters

mm = millimeters   cm = centimeters   m = meters

CHANGING INCHES TO MILLIMETERS AND CENTIMETERS
(Slightly rounded for your convenience.)

inches	mm	cm	inches	cm	inches	cm
1/8	3mm		7		29	73.5
1/4	6mm		8	20.5	30	76
3/8	10mm or	1cm	9	23	31	79
1/2	13mm or	1.3cm	10	25.5	32	81.5
5/8	15mm or	1.5cm	11	28	33	84
3/4	20mm or	2cm	12	30.5	34	86.5
7/8	22mm or	2.2cm	13	33	35	89
1	25mm or	2.5cm	14	35.5	36	91.5
1 1/4	32mm or	3.2cm	15	38	37	94
1 1/2	38mm or	3.8cm	16	40.5	38	96.5
1 3/4	45mm or	4.5cm	17	43	39	99
2	50mm or	5cm	18	46	40	101.5
2 1/2	65mm or	6.5cm	19	48.5	41	104
3	75mm or	7.5cm	20	51	42	106.5
3 1/2	90mm or	9cm	21	53.5	43	109
4	100mm or	10cm	22	56	44	112
4 1/2	115mm or	11.5cm	23	58.5	45	114.5
5	125mm or	12.5cm	24	61	46	117
5 1/2	140mm or	14cm	25	63.5	47	119.5
6	150mm or	15cm	26	66	48	122
			27	68.5	49	124.5
			28	71	50	127

Index